MW00510195

Greek Cookbook

125 Mediterranean Recipes to Enjoy The Authentic Food of The Greek Islands at Your Home

Linda Worley

SPECIAL DISCLAIMER

All the information's included in this book are given for instructive, informational and entertainment purposes, the author can claim to share very good quality recipes but is not headed for the perfect data and uses of the mentioned recipes, in fact the information's are not intent to provide dietary advice without a medical consultancy.

The author does not hold any responsibility for errors, omissions or contrary interpretation of the content in this book.

It is recommended to consult a medical practitioner before to approach any kind of diet, especially if you have a particular health situation, the author isn't headed for the responsibility of these situations and everything is under the responsibility of the reader, the author strongly recommend to preserve the health taking all precautions to ensure ingredients are fully cooked.

All the trademarks and brands used in this book are only mentioned to clarify the sources of the information's and to describe better a topic and all the trademarks and brands mentioned own their copyrights and they are not related in any way to this document and to the author.

This document is written to clarify all the information's of publishing purposes and cover any possible issue.

This document is under copyright and it is not possible to reproduce any part of this content in every kind of digital or printable document. All rights reserved.

© Copyright 2021 Linda Worley. All rights reserved.

Introduction

This complete greek cookbook offers you 125 best dishes from Greek cuisine.

There are a lot of traditional recipes included in this manuscript, well-balanced, delicious and nutritious dishes for everyday cooking.

Meat, poultry and seafood options, Greek Food is known as one of the best Mediterranean Food and this cookbook offers also many vegetarian Greek recipes..

The particularity of this book is that the recipes are simple, tasty, and the ingredients are widely accessible.

You don't need to be an experienced chef either to enjoy the benefits of this cookbook.

From mouth-watering soups, warm and cold salads to many pastas specialities, the delicious flavors will satisfy everyone who will try these recipes.

Enjoy the taste of a new culture with this Greek Cookbook!

Table Of Contents

Greek Pasta	1
Greek Squid (Soupies)	2
Gigantes (Greek Lima Beans)	3
Greek Pita Pizzas	4
Greek Chicken Pitas	5
Greek Orzo with Feta	6
Greek Butter Cookies	7
Classic Greek Spinach	8
Greek Chicken Burgers with Feta	9
Greek Style Garlic Chicken Breast	10
Greek Pizzas	11
Amazing Greek Pasta	12
Greek Garbanzo Bean Salad	13
Ali's Greek Tortellini Salad	14
Best Greek Stuffed Turkey	15
Greek Pasta Salad	16
Greek Lentil Salad	17
Grilled Greek-Style Zucchini	18
Greek Goddess Pasta Salad	19
Greek-alicious Pasta Salad	20
Greek Salad III	21
Greek Orzo and Broccoli	22
Greek Salad Dip	23
Greek Chicken Kozani	24
Greek Salad I	25
Greek Pasta Salad	26
Keftedes - Greek Meatballs	27
Greek Salad IV	28
Loaded Greek Burgers	29
Greek Chicken Stew (Stifado)	30
Quick Greek Pasta Salad with Steak	31
Greek Souvlaki Dressing	32
Greek Hero	33
Greek Scrambled Eggs	34
Greek Burgers	35

Table Of Contents

Greek Chicken Pasta	36
Greek-Style Rib Eye Steaks	37
Greek Pizza with Spinach, Feta and Olives	38
Greek Chicken	39
Greek Chicken Salad	40
Greek Traditional Turkey with Chestnut and Pine Nut Stuffing	41
Greek Salad II	42
Margaret's Keftedes (Greek Meatballs)	43
Greek Grilled Cheese	44
Tina's Greek Stuffed Peppers	45
Greek Easter Cookies from Smyrna	46
Pennsylvania Greek Sauce	47
Greek Veggie Salad	48
Greek Stuffed Peppers	49
Greek Loaf	50
Spanakopita (Greek Spinach Pie)	51
Greek Honey Cake	52
Sofrito (Greek Lamb Recipe)	53
Octapodi Kokkinisto (Greek Octopus in Tomato Sauce)	54
Greek Avocado Relish with Grilled Lamb Kebabs	55
Sheila's Greek Style Avocado Dip	56
Oven Roasted Greek Potatoes	57
Easy Greek Skillet Dinner	58
Fran's Greek Butter Cookies	59
Greek Potato Stew	60
Greek-Style Baked Salmon	61
Greek Lamb Kabobs with Yogurt-Mint Salsa Verde	62
Briam (Greek Mixed Vegetables in Tomato Sauce)	63
Greek Dip	64
Greek Olive and Onion Bread	65
Greek-Style Green Beans	66
Greek Spaghetti	67
Greek Salad V	68
Greek Pork Cutlets	69
Greek Chicken Wrap	70

Table Of Contents

Marinated Greek Chicken Kabobs	71
Greek Lemon Chicken Soup	72
Easy Greek Yogurt Cucumber Sauce	73
Greek Tomatoes	74
Warm Greek Pita Sandwiches With Turkey and Cucumber-Yogurt	75
Greek Rice Salad	76
Party-Size Greek Couscous Salad	77
Greek Souzoukaklia	78
Greek Pasta with Tomatoes and White Beans	79
Oia Greek Salad	80
Taramousalata (Greek Caviar Spread)	81
Greek Pasta and Beef	82
Greek Garlic-Lemon Potatoes	83
Greek Veggie Salad II	84
Vaselopita - Greek New Years Cake	85
Greek Orzo Salad	86
Greek Bifteki	87
Greek Orange Roast Lamb	88
A Lot More Than Plain Spinach Pie (Greek Batsaria)	89
Standard Greek Salad	90
Mediterranean Greek Salad	91
Greek Burgers	92
Swanson ® Greek-Style Beef Stew	93
Greek Egg Biscuits	94
Greek Spaghetti II	95
Greek Lentil Soup (Fakes)	96
Greek Pasta Salad with Roasted Vegetables and Feta	97
Greek Chicken	98
Absolutely Fabulous Greek/House Dressing	99
Grilled Mediterranean Greek Pizza with Sundried Tomato Chicken	100
Greek Tomato Salad	101
Greek Stuffed Tomatoes	102
Greek Pasta Salad II	103
Frozen Greek Yogurt	104
Good for You Greek Salad	105

Table Of Contents

Stuffed Bell Peppers, Greek Style	106
Greeked Zucchini	107
Greek Steffotto	108
My Big Fat Greek Omelet	109
Greek Green Beans	110
Greek Shrimp Dish From Santorini	111
Kourambiathes (Greek Cookies)	112
George's Greek Fried Chicken	113
Greek Saganaki	114
Greek Feta And Olive Spread	115
Greek Lamb Kabobs	116
Two Layer Greek Dip	117
Herbed Greek Roasted Potatoes with Feta Cheese	118
Greek Pasta Salad III	119
Greek Seasoning	120
Greek God Pasta	121
Greek Sausage: Sheftalia	122
Greek-Style Stuffed Peppers	123
Cousin Cosmo's Greek Chicken	124
Greek Orzo Salad	125

Greek Pasta

Ingredients

1 pound linguine pasta
3 tomatoes
1/3 cup olive oil
3 cloves garlic, minced
1 pound mushrooms, sliced
1 teaspoon dried oregano
3/4 cup crumbled feta cheese
1 (2 ounce) can sliced black
olives, drained

Directions

Bring a large pot of lightly salted water to a boil. Plunge whole tomatoes in water briefly, until skin starts to peel. Remove with a slotted spoon and place in cold water. Add pasta to boiling water and cook for 8 to 10 minutes or until al dente; drain.

While pasta is cooking peel blanched tomatoes and chop.

In a large skillet over medium heat, heat olive oil. Stir in garlic and mushrooms and saute until mushrooms begin to give up their juices. Stir in tomatoes and oregano and cook until tomatoes are tender.

To serve, plate pasta, top with hot tomato sauce and sprinkle with feta and olives.

Greek Squid (Soupies)

Ingredients

2 pounds squid - tentacles and tubes, cleaned and cut into chunks
2 medium onions, finely chopped
2 bay leaves
5 whole cloves
1 (3 inch) cinnamon stick
2 cups dry red wine
1/3 cup olive oil
1/3 cup malt vinegar
1/4 teaspoon ground black pepper

Directions

Place the squid and onions into a large saucepan with the cinnamon stick, cloves, and bay leaves. Cover, and simmer over low heat for about 10 minutes. During this time the squid will release its juices. Uncover the pan, and simmer until the juice has mostly evaporated. Remove the cinnamon stick, cloves, and bay leaves.

Stir in the wine, olive oil, malt vinegar and pepper. Cover and cook over low heat for about 1 hour, stirring occasionally. If necessary, remove the lid shortly before the end of cooking to allow the sauce to thicken. Ladle into bowls to serve.

Gigantes (Greek Lima Beans)

Ingredients

1 (16 ounce) package dried lima beans
2 (16 ounce) cans chopped tomatoes with juice
1 cup olive oil
3 cloves garlic, chopped
sea salt to taste
1 teaspoon chopped fresh dill

Directions

Place the lima beans in a large saucepan. Pour enough water to fill to 2 inches above top of the beans. Allow to soak overnight.

Preheat oven to 375 degrees F (190 degrees C).

Place the saucepan over medium heat; bring to a boil; reduce heat to medium-low and simmer 20 minutes; drain. Pour the beans into a 9 x 13 baking dish. Add the tomatoes, olive oil, garlic, salt, and dill; stir.

Bake in preheated oven for 1 1/2 to 2 hours, stirring occasionally and adding water if the mixture appears dry.

Greek Pita Pizzas

Ingredients

2 whole pita breads
2 tablespoons olive or vegetable oil, divided
1/4 cup sliced stuffed olives
2 teaspoons red wine vinegar or cider vinegar
1 garlic clove, minced
1/2 teaspoon dried oregano
1/4 teaspoon dried basil
Dash pepper
1/2 cup torn fresh spinach
1/3 cup crumbled feta cheese
1 small tomato, seeded and chopped
1/4 cup shredded Parmesan cheese

Directions

Brush pitas with 1 tablespoon oil. Place on a baking sheet. Broil 4 in. from the heat for 2 minutes. Meanwhile, in a bowl, combine the olives, vinegar, garlic, oregano, basil, pepper and remaining oil. Spread over pitas; top with spinach, feta cheese, tomato and Parmesan cheese. Broil 3 minutes longer or until cheese is melted.

Ingredients

1 medium onion, diced
3 cloves garlic, minced
1 pound skinless, boneless
chicken breast halves - cut into
strips
1 teaspoon lemon pepper 1/2
teaspoon dried oregano 1/4
teaspoon allspice
1/4 cup plain yogurt
1/4 cup sour cream
1/2 cup cucumber, peeled and
diced
4 pita bread rounds, cut in half

Directions

Place onion and garlic in a slow cooker. Season chicken with lemon pepper, oregano, and allspice; place on top of onions.

Cover, and cook on High for 6 hours.

In a small bowl, stir together yogurt, sour cream, and cucumber. Refrigerate until chicken is done cooking.

When chicken is done, fill pita halves with chicken, and top with the yogurt sauce.

Greek Orzo with Feta

Ingredients

1/4 cup olive oil
1/2 cup fresh lemon juice
1/2 cup pitted kalamata olives, chopped
2 ripe tomatoes, seeded and diced
1 red bell pepper, chopped
1 red onion, chopped
2 cloves garlic, minced
1 teaspoon finely chopped fresh oregano
1 (8 ounce) package crumbled feta cheese
1/2 pound dried orzo pasta
1 cup chopped fresh parsley

Directions

Stir together olive oil, lemon juice, olives, tomatoes, red pepper, red onion, garlic, oregano, and feta cheese in a large bowl. Let stand at room temperature for 1 hour.

Bring a large pot of lightly salted water to a boil. Add the orzo and cook for 8 to 10 minutes or until al dente; drain and toss the tomato mixture. Sprinkle with chopped parsley to serve.

Greek Butter Cookies

Ingredients

1 cup butter, softened
3/4 cup white sugar
1 egg
1/2 teaspoon vanilla extract
1/2 teaspoon almond extract
2 1/4 cups all-purpose flour
1/2 cup confectioners' sugar for rolling

Directions

Preheat the oven to 400 degrees F (200 degrees C). Grease cookie sheets.

In a medium bowl, cream together the butter, sugar and egg until smooth. Stir in the vanilla and almond extracts. Blend in the flour to form a dough. you may have to knead by hand at the end. Take about a teaspoon of dough at a time and roll into balls, logs or 'S' shapes. Place cookies 1 to 2 inches apart onto the prepared cookie sheets.

Bake for 10 minutes in the preheated oven, or until lightly browned and firm. Allow cookies to cool completely before dusting with confectioners' sugar.

Classic Greek Spinach

Ingredients

1 cup olive oil
2 onions, chopped
1 (10 ounce) package frozen chopped spinach, thawed and drained
2 large tomatoes, coarsely chopped
3 cups water
1 clove garlic, minced
1 tablespoon tomato paste
1 cube beef bouillon
salt and pepper to taste
1/2 cup uncooked long-grain white rice

Directions

Heat olive oil in a medium saucepan over medium heat. Stir in onions, and cook until tender. Mix in spinach. Stir in tomatoes. Allow vegetables to simmer about 5 minutes

Pour 2 cups water into saucepan, and bring to a boil. Mix in garlic, tomato paste, bouillon cube, salt and pepper. Reduce heat, and cook at a low boil about 15 minutes, until water is reduced by half.

Stir rice and remaining water into the spinach mixture. Return to boil, reduce heat , and simmer covered 20 minutes, or until rice is tender and fluffy.

Greek Chicken Burgers with Feta

Ingredients

1 pound ground chicken
1/2 cup dry bread crumbs
1 egg
1 tablespoon lemon juice
2 tablespoons chopped sun-dried tomatoes
1 tablespoon chopped fresh basil
3 teaspoons chopped fresh oregano
salt and pepper to taste
2 ounces crumbled feta cheese

Directions

Preheat an outdoor grill for medium-high heat, and lightly oil the grate.

Mix the chicken, bread crumbs, egg, lemon juice, sun-dried tomatoes, basil, oregano, salt, and pepper together in a bowl; form the mixture into 5 patties. Divide the feta cheese between the 5 patties; place a portion of the feta cheese atop each patty and fold the chicken mixture around the cheese so that the cheese is in the center.

Cook on the preheated grill until no longer pink on the inside and the juices run clear, 5 to 7 minutes per side. An instant-read thermometer inserted into the center should read 165 degrees F (75 degrees C).

Greek Style Garlic Chicken Breast

ngredients

- skinless, boneless chicken reast halves
- cup extra virgin olive oil
- lemon, juiced
- teaspoons crushed garlic
- teaspoon salt
- 1/2 teaspoons black pepper
- /3 teaspoon paprika

Directions

Cut 3 slits in each chicken breast to allow marinade to penetrate. In a small bowl, whisk together olive oil, lemon juice, garlic, salt, pepper, and paprika for about 30 seconds. Place chicken in a large bowl, and pour marinade over. Using your hands, work marinade into chicken. Cover, and refrigerate overnight.

Preheat grill for medium heat, and lightly oil grate.

Cook chicken on grill until meat is no longer pink and juices run clear.

Ingredients

4 (6 inch) pita breads
1 cup reduced-fat ricotta cheese
1/2 teaspoon garlic powder
1 (10 ounce) package frozen chopped spinach, thawed and squeezed dry
3 medium tomatoes, sliced 3/4 cup crumbled feta cheese 3/4 teaspoon dried basil

Directions

Place pita breads on a baking sheet. Combine the ricotta cheese and garlic powder; spread over pitas. Top with spinach, tomatoes, feta cheese and basil. Bake at 400 degrees F for 12-15 minutes or until bread is lightly browned.

ngredients

small yellow onion, diced
tablespoon olive oil
 cloves garlic, minced
 (16 ounce) can organic Italian
diced tomatoes
 (6.5 ounce) can tomato sauce
 tablespoon capers, chopped
15 kalamata olives, pitted and
sliced
2 tablespoons balsamic vinegar
salt and pepper to taste
crushed red pepper to taste
(optional)
crumbled Feta or grated
Parmesan Cheese

Directions

In a skillet, cook onion in olive oil over medium high heat until tender and translucent. Stir in garlic, and cook for 1 minute. Add tomatoes, tomato sauce, capers, olives, vinegar, salt, pepper, and crushed red pepper (if using).

Reduce heat, cover, and simmer for a minimum of 30 minutes, or up to 2 hours, time permitting. Serve over pasta, fish, or chicken, and top with crumbled feta or grated Parmesan cheese. Enjoy!

Greek Garbanzo Bean Salad

Ingredients

2 (15 ounce) cans garbanzo beans, drained
2 cucumbers, halved lengthwise and sliced
12 cherry tomatoes, halved
1/2 red onion, chopped
2 cloves garlic, minced
1 (15 ounce) can black olives, drained and chopped
1 ounce crumbled feta cheese
1/2 cup Italian-style salad dressing
1/2 lemon, juiced
1/2 teaspoon garlic salt
1/2 teaspoon ground black pepper

Directions

Combine the beans, cucumbers, tomatoes, red onion, garlic, olives, cheese, salad dressing, lemon juice, garlic salt and pepper. Toss together and refrigerate 2 hours before serving. Serve chilled.

Ali's Greek Tortellini Salad

Ingredients

(9 ounce) packages cheese
tortellini
/2 cup extra virgin olive oil
/4 cup lemon juice
/4 cup red wine vinegar
tablespoons chopped fresh
parsley
teaspoon dried oregano
/2 teaspoon salt
eggs
pound baby spinach leaves
cup crumbled feta cheese
/2 cup slivered red onion

Directions

Bring a large pot of lightly salted water to a boil. Add tortellini, and cook for 7 minutes or until al dente; drain.

In a large bowl, mix the olive oil, lemon juice, red wine vinegar, parsley, oregano, and salt. Place the cooked tortellini in the bowl, and toss to coat. Cover, and chill at least 2 hours in the refrigerator.

Place eggs in a saucepan with enough water to cover, and bring to a boil. Remove from heat, and allow eggs to sit in the hot water for 10 to 12 minutes. Drain, cool, peel, and quarter.

Gently mix the spinach, feta cheese, and onion into the bowl with the pasta. Arrange the quartered eggs around the salad to serve.

Best Greek Stuffed Turkey

Ingredients

1 (12 pound) whole turkey, thawed
3 lemons, juiced
1/4 cup butter
4 medium onions, chopped
2 turkey livers, finely chopped
1 pound ground lamb
2 1/2 cups long grain white rice
1 tablespoon ground cinnamon
1/4 cup chopped fresh mint leaves
2 tablespoons tomato paste
3 cups water
salt and pepper to taste
1/2 cup butter, melted

Directions

Preheat the oven to 450 degrees F (230 degrees C). Rinse the turkey inside and out, and pat dry with paper towels. Rub lemon juice all over the turkey and inside the cavity. Set aside.

Melt 1/4 cup of butter in a large skillet over medium heat. Add the onion, and cook for about 5 minutes, until tender. Add the chopped livers and ground lamb. Cook, stirring to crumble, until evenly browned. Stir in the rice, cinnamon, mint and tomato paste. Mix in 1 cup of the water, and season with salt and pepper. Cook over low heat for 10 minutes, stirring constantly.

Fill turkey with the stuffing mixture, and truss. Place on a rack in a shallow roasting pan, and pour the remaining 2 cups of water into the pan. Mix together the remaining lemon juice and melted butter. This is the basting sauce.

Bake for 1 hour in the preheated oven, then reduce the temperature of the oven to 350 degrees F (175 degrees C) and continue roasting for 2 more hours, or until the internal temperature of the thickest part of the thigh reaches 180 degrees F (80 degrees C). Baste occasionally with the melted butter and lemon juice.

Greek Pasta Salad

Ingredients

(16 ounce) package penne pasta
/4 cup vegetable oil
teaspoon lemon juice
teaspoon dried basil
teaspoon ground black pepper
teaspoon garlic salt
tomatoes, chopped
green bell pepper, chopped
sweet onion, chopped
cucumber, coarsely chopped
cup black olives, chopped

Directions

Cook pasta in a large pot of boiling water until al dente. Drain, and rinse in cold water.

In a small bowl, mix together oil, lemon juice, basil, garlic salt, and black pepper.

In a large bowl, combine pasta, tomatoes, green pepper, onion, cucumber, and black olives. Add dressing, and toss to coat. Chill in the refrigerator for 30 minutes.

Greek Lentil Salad

Ingredients

2 (15 ounce) cans brown lentils
1 cup crumbled feta cheese
1/2 (16 ounce) bottle Greek, or other vinaigrette salad dressing
1 English cucumber, peeled and diced
1 beefsteak tomato, diced
1 large red onion, diced

Directions

Strain lentils and place in a large bowl. Pour in 1/2 of the salad dressing, and stir to coat. Place in the refrigerator while preparing other vegetables. Add feta cheese, cucumber, tomato, and red onion. Cover, and refrigerate for 1 hour.

Stir in remaining dressing when ready to serve. May be kept, covered, in the refrigerator for up to 3 days.

Grilled Greek-Style Zucchini

Ingredients

- small zucchini, thinly sliced
- medium tomato, seeded and chopped
- 1/4 cup pitted ripe olives, halved
- 2 tablespoons chopped green onion
- 4 teaspoons olive or canola oil
- 2 teaspoons lemon juice 1/2
- easpoon dried oregano 1/2
- easpoon garlic salt 1/4
- easpoon pepper
- 2 tablespoons grated Parmesan cheese

Directions

In a bowl, combine the zucchini, tomato, olives and onion. Combine oil, lemon juice, oregano, garlic salt and pepper; pour over vegetables and toss to coat. Place on a double thickness of heavy-duty foil (about 23 in. x 18 in.). Fold foil around vegetables and seal tightly. Grill, covered, over medium heat for 10-15 minutes or until vegetables are tender. Sprinkle with Parmesan cheese.

Greek Goddess Pasta Salad

Ingredients

1 (12 ounce) package tri-colored rotini pasta
1 small head broccoli, broken into small florets
1/2 teaspoon minced garlic
1 small red onion, diced
1 (12 ounce) jar marinated artichoke hearts, drained and chopped
1 (12 ounce) jar pitted kalamata olives, sliced
1 (8 ounce) jar roasted red bell peppers, drained, cut into strips
4 Roma tomatoes, diced
1 (12 ounce) jar oil-packed sun-dried tomatoes, drained, cut into strips
1 small zucchini, chopped
1 small cucumber, chopped
1 small yellow bell pepper, chopped
2 ripe avocados
1 (16 ounce) bottle Greek vinaigrette salad dressing

Directions

Fill a large pot with lightly salted water and bring to a rolling boil over high heat. Once the water is boiling, stir in the pasta, and return to a boil. Cook the pasta uncovered, stirring occasionally, until the pasta has cooked through, but is still firm to the bite, about 10 minutes. Drain well in a colander set in the sink, rinse with cool water and place in a large bowl.

Place a steamer insert into a saucepan, and fill with water to just below the bottom of the steamer. Cover, and bring the water to a boil over high heat. Add the broccoli , recover, and steam until just tender, 2 to 6 minutes depending on thickness. Rinse the broccoli with cold water, finely chop, and add to pasta.

Stir in the garlic, red onion, artichoke hearts, kalamata olives, roasted red peppers, Roma tomatoes, sun-dried tomatoes, zucchini, cucumber, and yellow pepper and combine well.

Cut the avocados in half, remove the pit, and remove from the skin with a large spoon. Cut the avocados into large pieces, place in a small bowl and mash well with a fork. Slowly whisk in the Greek dressing until well combined. Pour the Greek-avocado dressing into the pasta salad and gently toss. Refrigerate for at least one hour before serving.

Greek-alicious Pasta Salad

Ingredients

- 1/2 cups bow tie (farfalle) pasta
- cup Greek salad dressing
- 1/2 tablespoons mayonnaise
- radishes, finely chopped
- /2 cucumber, peeled and chopped
- (15 ounce) can garbanzo beans, drained
- 3/4 cup crumbled feta cheese

Directions

Fill a large pot with lightly salted water and bring to a rolling boil over high heat. Once the water is boiling, stir in the bow tie pasta and return to a boil. Cook the pasta uncovered, stirring occasionally, until the pasta has cooked through, but is still firm to the bite, about 12 minutes. Drain well in a colander set in the sink.

Place the Greek dressing and mayonnaise into a large salad bowl, and whisk together until smooth and well blended. Add the cooked pasta, and stir lightly to coat the pasta. Sprinkle on the radishes, cucumber, garbanzo beans, and crumbled feta cheese, and fold in gently.

Cover the salad and refrigerate until ready to serve.

Greek Salad III

Ingredients

3 roma (plum) tomatoes, chopped
1 green bell pepper, sliced
1 small English cucumber, chopped
1 small onion, chopped
1/4 cup sliced black olives (optional)
2 ounces tomato basil feta cheese, crumbled
1/4 cup olive oil
1 teaspoon red wine vinegar
1 teaspoon lemon juice
1 clove garlic, minced
1/2 teaspoon dried oregano
salt and pepper to taste

Directions

In a salad bowl, combine the tomatoes, bell pepper, cucumber, onion and olives.

Whisk together the oil, vinegar, lemon juice, garlic, oregano, salt and pepper. Let sit for 1 hour, occasionally stirring to blend flavors.

Pour dressing over salad, add feta cheese and toss before serving.

Greek Orzo and Broccoli

Ingredients

3/4 cup uncooked orzo pasta
2 cups fresh broccoli florets
1/3 cup pitted Greek olives
1/4 cup crumbled feta cheese
1/4 cup grated Parmesan cheese
2 tablespoons minced fresh basil
1 1/2 teaspoons toasted slivered almonds
1 tablespoon olive oil
1/4 teaspoon crushed red pepper flakes
1/4 teaspoon pepper

Directions

In a large saucepan, cook pasta in boiling water for 7 minutes. Add broccoli and cook 2-3 minutes longer or until pasta is tender; drain. Meanwhile, in a small bowl, combine the olives, feta cheese, Parmesan cheese and basil.

In a small nonstick skillet, saute almonds in oil for about 1 minute. Stir in red pepper flakes and pepper; cook and stir 1 minute longer. Pour over pasta mixture; toss to coat. Stir in olive mixture; toss to coat.

Ingredients

8 ounces crumbled feta cheese
1 (2.25 ounce) can chopped black olives
1 tomatoes, seeded and chopped
3 green onions, finely chopped
1/2 cup Caesar salad dressing

Directions

Mix the feta cheese, olives, tomatoes, green onions, and Caesar salad dressing in a bowl. Chill 25 minutes in the refrigerator.

Greek Chicken Kozani

Ingredients

4 skinless chicken thighs
4 cups water
3 tablespoons olive oil
3 large red onions, halved, then sliced lengthwise
20 pitted prunes
1 1/2 tablespoons sweet paprika
2 bay leaves
1 tablespoon salt, or to taste
ground black pepper to taste

Directions

Place the chicken thighs and water into a saucepan. Bring to a boil over high heat, then reduce heat to medium-low, and simmer 10 to 15 minutes. Skim off any foam that floats to the surface.

Meanwhile, heat the olive oil in a large skillet over low heat. Stir in the onions, and cook covered until soft and translucent, about 10 minutes. Do not let the onions brown. Add the chicken to the onions along with 3 cups of the cooking liquid. Stir in the prunes, paprika, bay leaves, salt, and pepper. Return to a simmer, cover, and cook until the prunes are tender and the flavors have combined, 15 to 25 minutes.

Ingredients

1 head romaine lettuce- rinsed, dried and chopped
1 red onion, thinly sliced
1 (6 ounce) can pitted black olives
1 green bell pepper, chopped
1 red bell pepper, chopped
2 large tomatoes, chopped
1 cucumber, sliced
1 cup crumbled feta cheese
6 tablespoons olive oil
1 teaspoon dried oregano
1 lemon, juiced
ground black pepper to taste

Directions

In a large salad bowl, combine the Romaine, onion, olives, bell peppers, tomatoes, cucumber and cheese.

Whisk together the olive oil, oregano, lemon juice and black pepper. Pour dressing over salad, toss and serve.

Greek Pasta Salad

Ingredients

(16 ounce) package penne pasta
/4 cup vegetable oil
teaspoon lemon juice
teaspoon dried basil
teaspoon ground black pepper
teaspoon garlic salt
tomatoes, chopped
green bell pepper, chopped
sweet onion, chopped
cucumber, coarsely chopped
cup black olives, chopped

Directions

Cook pasta in a large pot of boiling water until al dente. Drain, and rinse in cold water.

In a small bowl, mix together oil, lemon juice, basil, garlic salt, and black pepper.

In a large bowl, combine pasta, tomatoes, green pepper, onion, cucumber, and black olives. Add dressing, and toss to coat. Chill in the refrigerator for 30 minutes.

Keftedes - Greek Meatballs

Ingredients

oil for frying
1/4 cup fresh lemon juice
5 white potatoes, peeled
2 pounds ground beef
1 large onion, grated
3/4 cup dry bread crumbs
1 cup chopped fresh parsley
1/3 cup dried mint, crushed
1/2 teaspoon ground cinnamon
zest from 1 lemon
2 eggs, beaten
1 1/2 tablespoons salt
1 teaspoon ground black pepper
lemon wedges

Directions

Heat oil in a deep-fryer or large saucepan to 325 degrees F (165 degrees C).

Place the lemon juice in a large bowl. Coarsely grate the potatoes into the lemon juice, stirring well to prevent browning. Stir in the ground beef, onion, bread crumbs, parsley, mint, cinnamon, lemon zest, eggs, and salt and pepper. Mix well, and shape into oblong balls about 1 inch thick and 2 inches wide.

Place meatballs in hot oil in batches; do not crowd. Fry until golden brown, and cooked through, about 6 to 7 minutes per batch. Serve with lemon wedges.

ngredients

large tomatoes, chopped
green bell pepper, chopped
cucumber, peeled and chopped
red onion, chopped
ounces crumbled feta cheese
/4 cup olive oil
/8 cup lemon juice

Directions

In a large bowl, combine the tomatoes, green bell pepper, cucumber, red onion, olive oil, and lemon juice. Refrigerate until thoroughly chilled. Sprinkle with feta cheese before serving.

Loaded Greek Burgers

Ingredients

1 red bell pepper

Spread:
2 ounces crumbled feta cheese
2 tablespoons mayonnaise
2 teaspoons lime juice
1 sprig fresh mint, chopped
1 sprig fresh parsley, chopped

Burgers:
1 pound lean ground beef
6 ounces crumbled feta cheese
8 ounces fresh spinach - rinsed,
drained and coarsely chopped
1/4 cup bread crumbs
1 egg
1 clove garlic, minced
1/4 cup chopped onion
2 sprigs fresh basil, coarsely
chopped
3 sprigs fresh mint, coarsely
chopped
2 sprigs fresh parsley, coarsely
chopped
salt and ground black pepper to
taste
4 Kaiser rolls, split and toasted
1 tomato, sliced
4 leaves lettuce

Directions

Preheat the oven's broiler and set the oven rack about 6 inches from the heat source. Line a baking sheet with aluminum foil. Cut the red bell pepper in half from top to bottom; remove the stem, seeds, and ribs; place pepper cut-side-down onto the prepared baking sheet.

Cook under the preheated broiler until the skin of the pepper has blackened and blistered, about 5 minutes. Allow the blackened pepper to cool and steam in a paper bag for 5 minutes; peel and dice; set aside.

Stir together the 2 ounces feta cheese, mayonnaise, lime juice, the 1 sprig chopped mint, and the 1 sprig chopped parsley in a small bowl; set aside.

Preheat an outdoor grill for medium heat, and lightly oil the grate.

Place the roasted red pepper, ground beef, feta cheese, spinach, bread crumbs, egg, garlic, onion, basil, the remaining mint, and the remaining parsley in a bowl. Sprinkle with salt and pepper, and mix gently with your hands until evenly combined. Divide the meat mixture to form 4 equal 4 1/2 inch patties.

Cook on the preheated grill until the burgers are cooked to your desired degree of doneness, about 4 minutes per side for medium. An instant-read thermometer inserted into the center should read 160 degrees F (70 degrees C). Serve burgers on warm toasted Kaiser roll with the feta cheese spread, fresh tomatoes, and lettuce.

Greek Chicken Stew (Stifado)

ngredients

0 small shallots, peeled
 cup olive oil
 teaspoons butter
 (4 pound) whole chicken, cut
nto pieces
 cloves garlic, finely chopped
1/2 cup red wine
 cup tomato sauce
 tablespoons chopped fresh
arsley
alt and ground black pepper to
aste
 pinch dried oregano, or to taste
 bay leaves
 1/2 cups chicken stock, or more
f needed

Directions

Bring a large pot of lightly salted water to a boil. Add the shallots, and cook uncovered for 3 minutes until just tender. Drain in a colander, then immediately immerse in ice water, or rinse with cold water for several minutes until cold to stop the cooking process. Once the shallots are cold, drain well, and set aside.

Heat the olive oil and butter in a Dutch oven or large pot over medium heat until oil is hot and butter is melted and bubbling. Add the whole, blanched shallots and chicken pieces to the skillet and cook, turning chicken pieces over until no longer pink inside and shallots have softened and turned translucent, about 15 minutes. Stir in the chopped garlic and cook for another 3 minutes, until garlic starts to turn golden.

Pour in red wine and tomato sauce, and add the parsley, salt and pepper, oregano, and bay leaves. Pour the chicken stock over the chicken pieces to cover, and stir to combine.

Simmer the stew, covered, over medium-low heat for about 50 minutes, until the shallots are soft and the chicken is tender.

Quick Greek Pasta Salad with Steak

Ingredients

8 ounces whole wheat penne pasta
2 tablespoons extra virgin olive oil

1 tablespoon butter
1 (1 pound) beef rib eye steak
1 tablespoon butter
1 teaspoon minced garlic
1/4 cup chopped shallots
1 tablespoon soy sauce

1/2 cup sun-dried tomato pesto
1/2 cup sliced black olives
1 cup chopped fresh spinach
1 teaspoon basil
1 tablespoon chopped parsley
1/2 cup crumbled feta cheese
3 tablespoons sunflower kernels

Directions

Bring a large pot of lightly salted water to a boil. Add pasta and cook for 8 to 10 minutes or until al dente. When cooked, drain, then toss with olive oil, and keep warm.

Meanwhile, melt 1 tablespoon butter in a skillet over medium-high heat. Sear the rib-eye on both sides until rosy-pink in the center, 7 to 10 minutes depending on thickness. Remove steak from skillet and cut into bite-size pieces. Melt the remaining 1 tablespoon of butter in the skillet, and stir in the garlic and shallots. Cook 5 to 10 seconds until fragrant, then return the steak to the pan and cook for another 5 minutes or to desired doneness. Stir in the soy sauce, and cook a few seconds longer, allowing it to evaporate.

Remove the skillet from the heat and stir in the sun-dried tomato pesto, olives, spinach, basil, parsley, feta cheese and sunflower kernels. Toss with the pasta in a large bowl and serve.

Greek Souvlaki Dressing

Ingredients

tablespoons red wine vinegar
/2 clove minced garlic
/4 teaspoon dry mustard powder
pinch salt
pinch ground black pepper
teaspoons dried oregano, or to
aste
/2 cup extra virgin olive oil

Directions

Whisk together vinegar, garlic, mustard powder, salt, pepper, oregano, and olive oil together until blended. Pour into a glass dressing container, and allow to stand at least 2 hours before serving.

Ingredients

2 tablespoons lemon juice
1 tablespoon olive or canola oil
1 (15 ounce) can garbanzo beans or chickpeas, rinsed and drained
2 garlic cloves, minced
1 teaspoon dried oregano
1/4 teaspoon salt
1/8 teaspoon pepper
SANDWICH:
1 (8 ounce) loaf French baguette
2 medium sweet red peppers, cut into thin strips
1/2 medium cucumber, sliced
2 small tomatoes, sliced
1/4 cup thinly sliced red onion
1/4 cup chopped ripe olives
1/4 cup chopped pimento-stuffed olives
1/2 cup crumbled feta cheese
4 lettuce leaves

Directions

For hummus, place the lemon juice, oil and beans in a food processor; cover and process until smooth. Add garlic, oregano, salt and pepper; mix well.

Slice bread in half horizontally. Carefully hollow out bottom half, leaving a 1/2-in shell. Spread hummus into shell. Layer with the red peppers, cucumber, tomatoes, onion, olives, cheese and lettuce. Replace bread top. Cut into four portions.

Greek Scrambled Eggs

Ingredients

tablespoon butter
eggs
teaspoon water
/2 cup crumbled feta cheese
alt and pepper to taste

Directions

Heat butter in a skillet over medium-high heat. Beat eggs and water together, then pour into pan. Add feta cheese, and cook, stirring occasionally to scramble. Season with salt and pepper.

Ingredients

2 tablespoons 50% less fat feta cheese
1 pint low-fat plain yogurt or low-fat plain Greek yogurt
2 teaspoons fresh parsley
1/8 teaspoon lemon peel
1/8 teaspoon bottled minced garlic
1 Morningstar Farms® Grillers® Original
1 whole wheat or multi-grain hamburger bun
2 thin slices cucumber
1 thin slice red onion
1 1/2 teaspoons black olives

Directions

In a small bowl stir together feta cheese, yogurt, parsley, lemon peel and garlic. Cover and refrigerate until serving time.

Cook veggie burger according to package directions. Serve veggie burger on bun topped with yogurt mixture, cucumber, onion and olives.

Greek Chicken Pasta

Ingredients

1 pound uncooked pasta
1 tablespoon olive oil
2 cloves garlic, crushed
1/2 cup chopped red onion
1 pound skinless, boneless
chicken breast meat - cut into
bite-size pieces
1 (14 ounce) can marinated
artichoke hearts, drained and
chopped
1 large tomato, chopped
1/2 cup crumbled feta cheese
3 tablespoons chopped fresh
parsley
2 tablespoons lemon juice
2 teaspoons dried oregano
salt and pepper to taste
2 lemons, wedged, for garnish

Directions

Bring a large pot of lightly salted water to a boil. Cook pasta in boiling water for 8 to 10 minutes, or until al dente; drain.

Meanwhile, heat olive oil in a large skillet over medium-high heat. Add garlic and onion, and saute for 2 minutes. Stir in the chicken. Cook, stirring occasionally, until chicken is no longer pink and the juices run clear, about 5 to 6 minutes.

Reduce heat to medium-low, and add the artichoke hearts, tomato, feta cheese, parsley, lemon juice, oregano and cooked pasta. Stir until heated through, about 2 to 3 minutes. Remove from heat, season to taste with salt and pepper, and garnish with lemon wedges.

Greek-Style Rib Eye Steaks

Ingredients

1 1/2 teaspoons garlic powder
1 1/2 teaspoons dried oregano
1 1/2 teaspoons dried basil
1/2 teaspoon salt
1/8 teaspoon pepper
2 beef rib-eye steaks (1 1/2 inches thick)
1 tablespoon olive or vegetable oil
1 tablespoon lemon juice
2 tablespoons crumbled feta or blue cheese
1 tablespoon sliced ripe olives

Directions

In a small bowl, combine the first five ingredients;rub onto both sides of steaks. In a large skillet, cook steaks in oil for 7-9 minutes on each side or until meat reaches desired doneness (for medium-rare a meat thermometer should read 145 degrees F, medium, 160 degrees F, well-done, 170 degrees F). Sprinkle with lemon juice, cheese and olives. Serve immediately.

Greek Pizza with Spinach, Feta and Olives

Ingredients

/2 cup mayonnaise
 cloves garlic, minced
 cup crumbled feta cheese,
divided
 (12 inch) pre-baked Italian pizza
rust
/2 cup oil-packed sun-dried
omatoes, coarsely chopped
 tablespoon oil from the sun-
dried tomatoes
/4 cup pitted kalamata olives,
coarsely chopped
 teaspoon dried oregano
 cups baby spinach leaves 1/2
small red onion, halved and
thinly sliced

Directions

Adjust oven rack to lowest position, and heat oven to 450 degrees.
Mix mayonnaise, garlic and 1/2 cup feta in a small bowl. Place pizza
crust on a cookie sheet; spread mayonnaise mixture over pizza,
then top with tomatoes, olives and oregano. Bake until heated
through and crisp, about 10 minutes.

Toss spinach and onion with the 1 Tb. sun-dried tomato oil. Top hot
pizza with spinach mixture and remaining 1/2 cup feta cheese.
Return to oven and bake until cheese melts, about 2 minutes longer.
Cut into 6 slices and serve.

Greek Chicken

Ingredients

1/2 cup olive oil
3 cloves garlic, chopped
1 tablespoon chopped fresh rosemary
1 tablespoon chopped fresh thyme
1 tablespoon chopped fresh oregano
2 lemons, juiced
1 (4 pound) chicken, cut into pieces

Directions

In a glass dish, mix the olive oil, garlic, rosemary, thyme, oregano, and lemon juice. Place the chicken pieces in the mixture, cover, and marinate in the refrigerator 8 hours or overnight.

Preheat grill for high heat.

Lightly oil the grill grate. Place chicken on the grill, and discard the marinade. Cook chicken pieces up to 15 minutes per side, until juices run clear. Smaller pieces will not take as long.

Ingredients

cups cubed, cooked chicken
meat

/2 cup sliced carrots

/2 cup sliced cucumber

/4 cup sliced black olives

/4 cup crumbled feta cheese

/4 cup Italian-style salad
dressing

Directions

In a large bowl combine the chicken, carrots, cucumber, olives and cheese. Gently mix together. Add the salad dressing and mix well.

Cover and refrigerate. Let flavors marinate for at least 1 hour. Serve on a bed of lettuce if desired.

Greek Traditional Turkey with Chestnut and Pine

Ingredients

1 cup chestnuts
2/3 cup butter
1/4 cup orange juice 1/4
cup tangerine juice 2/3
cup lemon juice
1 (10 pound) whole turkey
salt and ground black pepper to
taste
1/2 pound ground beef
1/2 pound ground pork
1/4 cup chopped onion
1/2 cup uncooked instant rice
1/4 cup pine nuts
1/4 cup raisins (optional)
1/3 cup butter
1/2 cup chicken broth
2 tablespoons brandy
1 teaspoon salt
1/2 teaspoon ground black
pepper

Directions

Preheat oven to 325 degrees F (165 degrees C).

Make a small incision on sides of each chestnut, and place in a skillet over medium heat. Cook, stirring often, until toasted. Remove from heat, peel, and chop.

Melt 2/3 cup butter in a saucepan, and mix in the orange juice, tangerine juice, and lemon juice. Rub the turkey inside and out with the mixture, reserving some for basting. Season turkey with salt and pepper.

In a large skillet over medium heat, cook the ground beef, ground pork, and onion until beef and pork are evenly brown and onion is tender. Drain grease. Mix in the rice. Stir in the chestnuts, pine nuts, raisins, 1/3 cup butter, broth, and brandy. Season with 1 teaspoon salt and 1/2 teaspoon pepper. Continue cooking until all liquid has been absorbed. Stuff all turkey cavities with the mixture, and tie in place with kitchen twine.

Place turkey on a rack in a roasting pan, and loosely cover breast and thighs with aluminum foil. Pour about 1/4 inch water into the bottom of the pan. Maintain this level of water throughout cook time. Roast turkey in the preheated oven 3 to 4 hours, brushing occasionally with remaining butter and juice mixture. Increase oven temperature to 400 degrees F (200 degrees C) during final hour of roasting, and remove foil. Cook turkey to a minimum internal temperature of 180 degrees F (82 degrees C).

Ingredients

1 head romaine lettuce- rinsed, dried and chopped
4 stalks celery, chopped
1 onion, chopped
1 (15 ounce) can baby peas
2 ripe tomatoes, cut into wedges
5 ounces crumbled feta cheese
1 1/2 cups mayonnaise
1/2 cup vinaigrette salad dressing
5 ounces marinated chicken

Directions

Preheat grill to medium-high heat.

Remove chicken from marinade and drain. Place on hot grill and cook for 6 to 8 minutes on each side, or until juices run clear.

In a large bowl, combine Romaine, celery, onion, peas, tomatoes and toss with enough vinaigrette to coat.

In a food processor, add the crumbled feta and mayonnaise. Blend until smooth.

Place the tossed salad on a dinner plate and top with the feta mixture and grilled chicken or beef.

Margaret's Keftedes (Greek Meatballs)

Ingredients

4 slices white bread, torn into pieces
2 tablespoons milk
1 clove garlic
1 onion, quartered
4 teaspoons dried mint
1 teaspoon salt
ground black pepper to taste
1/2 pound ground beef
1/2 pound ground lamb
4 eggs
1/2 cup all-purpose flour for dredging
vegetable oil for frying

Directions

Moisten the bread pieces with the milk in a large bowl, and set aside. Mince the garlic in a food processor, then add the onion, mint, salt, and pepper. Process until the onion is finely chopped. Add the onion mixture to the bowl with the moist bread, along with the beef, lamb, and eggs. Mix with your hands until thoroughly blended.

Roll the mixture into balls measuring 1 1/2 to 2 inches in diameter. Place the flour in a shallow pan, and roll the balls in the flour to coat. Shake off any excess flour, and place the meatballs onto a plate or baking sheet, pressing to flatten slightly. This will keep them from rolling away.

Heat 1 inch of oil in a large skillet over medium heat. Add the meatballs, 8 or 10 at a time, and cook until nicely browned on the outside, and no longer pink in the center, about 10 minutes; drain on a paper towel-lined plate. Repeat with remaining meatballs.

Greek Grilled Cheese

Ingredients

1 1/2 teaspoons butter, softened
2 slices whole wheat bread, or
your favorite bread
2 tablespoons crumbled feta
cheese
2 slices Cheddar cheese
1 tablespoon chopped red onion
1/4 tomato, thinly sliced

Directions

Heat a skillet over medium heat. Butter one side of each slice of bread. On the non buttered side of one slice, layer the feta cheese, Cheddar cheese, red onion and tomato. Top with the other slice of bread with the butter side out.

Fry the sandwich until golden brown on each side, about 2 minutes per side. The second side always cooks faster.

Tina's Greek Stuffed Peppers

Ingredients

1/2 pound orzo pasta
2 tablespoons olive oil
1 yellow onion, chopped
2 large cloves garlic, chopped
1 1/2 pounds ground lamb
4 1/2 teaspoons dried oregano
1 tablespoon dried basil
salt and pepper to taste
1 (16 ounce) package frozen chopped spinach, thawed and drained
2 tomatoes, diced
1 (6 ounce) can tomato paste
8 ounces crumbled feta cheese
6 large green or red bell peppers - tops removed and seeded
olive oil

Directions

Bring a pot of lightly salted water to a boil over high heat. Cook the orzo in the boiling water uncovered, stirring occasionally, until tender yet firm to the bite, about 8 minutes. Drain.

Heat 2 tablespoons olive oil in a large skillet over medium high heat; cook and stir the onion and garlic in the hot oil until fragrant, about 1 minute. Crumble the ground lamb into the mixture; season with the oregano, basil, and salt and pepper. Continue cooking until the lamb is completely browned, 7 to 10 minutes. Remove from heat. Stir the orzo, spinach, tomatoes, tomato paste, and feta cheese into the lamb mixture until evenly incorporated.

Evenly rub the outside of the bell peppers and the tops with 2 tablespoons olive oil. Season with salt and pepper. Arrange in a baking dish large enough to accommodate all of them standing upright. Fill the peppers with the lamb mixture and replace the tops.

Roast in the preheated oven until the peppers begin to brown, 30 to 40 minutes.

Greek Easter Cookies from Smyrna

Ingredients

2 cups butter
1 1/2 cups white sugar
4 egg yolks
1/2 cup milk
5 cups sifted all-purpose flour
2 teaspoons baking powder
1 tablespoon orange zest
1 egg

Directions

Sift together flour and baking powder and set aside. In large bowl, cream together butter and sugar. Add 4 egg yolks one at a time, beating well after each one. Add milk and flour.

Work with the hands until dough is smooth. Add grated orange rind. Dough should be stiff so add additional flour if needed.

Break off small portions of dough and roll out into pencil-size strips about 11 inches long. Fold each strip into thirds, sideways, and press lightly together at ends.

Place cookies on ungreased baking sheet. Brush tops with beaten egg. Bake at 350 degrees F (175 degrees C) for 18 to 20 minutes.

Pennsylvania Greek Sauce

Ingredients

1 pound ground beef
2 small onions, chopped
1 (8 ounce) can tomato sauce
1 cup water
1/2 teaspoon salt
1/2 teaspoon ground black pepper
1/2 teaspoon dried oregano
1/2 teaspoon dried basil
1/2 teaspoon garlic powder
1/2 teaspoon ground cumin
1 teaspoon crushed red pepper flakes
2 teaspoons prepared yellow mustard

Directions

Place the beef in a large skillet over medium heat. Cook until beef is completely brown; drain. Stir the onions, tomato sauce, water, salt, pepper, oregano, basil, garlic powder, cumin, red pepper flakes, and yellow mustard into the beef. Bring to a boil; lower heat to medium-low and simmer 45 minutes, stirring occasionally.

Ingredients

1 head cauliflower, chopped
1 head broccoli, chopped
2 cups cherry tomatoes
1 (6 ounce) can small pitted black olives, drained
1 (6 ounce) package tomato basil feta cheese, crumbled
1 (16 ounce) bottle zesty Italian dressing

Directions

In a large bowl, combine the cauliflower, broccoli, cherry tomatoes, olives and cheese. Add enough dressing to coat, toss and refrigerate overnight.

Greek Stuffed Peppers

Ingredients

1 (8 ounce) package crumbled feta cheese
1 (2 ounce) jar chopped pimento peppers
1 teaspoon Greek seasoning
ground black pepper, to taste
1/4 cup olive oil
2 green bell peppers, cored and cut into quarters
8 slices bacon

Directions

Preheat oven to 400 degrees F (200 degrees C).

Stir the feta cheese, pimento peppers, Greek seasoning, black pepper, and olive oil together in a bowl; place about 2 tablespoons of the mixture on each of the 8 bell pepper segments. Wrap each segment with a slice of bacon; secure with toothpicks and arrange on a baking sheet.

Bake in the preheated oven until the bacon is brown and beginning to crisp, about 20 minutes. Serve hot.

Ingredients

cup milk (70 to 80 degrees F)
tablespoon olive or vegetable oil
teaspoon salt
3/4 cup crumbled feta cheese or shredded mozzarella cheese
cups bread flour
tablespoon sugar
2 1/4 teaspoons active dry yeast
1/4 cup sliced ripe olives

Directions

In bread machine pan, place the first seven ingredients in order suggested by manufacturer. Select basic bread setting. Choose crust color and loaf size if available. Bake according to bread machine directions (check dough after 5 minutes of mixing; add 1 to 2 tablespoons of water or flour if needed).

Just before the final kneading (your machine may audibly signal this), add the olives.

Spanakopita (Greek Spinach Pie)

Ingredients

3 tablespoons olive oil
1 large onion, chopped
1 bunch green onions, chopped
2 cloves garlic, minced
2 pounds spinach, rinsed and chopped
1/2 cup chopped fresh parsley
2 eggs, lightly beaten
1/2 cup ricotta cheese
1 cup crumbled feta cheese
8 sheets phyllo dough
1/4 cup olive oil

Directions

Preheat oven to 350 degrees F (175 degrees C). Lightly oil a 9x9 inch square baking pan.

Heat 3 tablespoons olive oil in a large skillet over medium heat. Saute onion, green onions and garlic, until soft and lightly browned. Stir in spinach and parsley, and continue to saute until spinach is limp, about 2 minutes. Remove from heat and set aside to cool.

In a medium bowl, mix together eggs, ricotta, and feta. Stir in spinach mixture. Lay 1 sheet of phyllo dough in prepared baking pan, and brush lightly with olive oil. Lay another sheet of phyllo dough on top, brush with olive oil, and repeat process with two more sheets of phyllo. The sheets will overlap the pan. Spread spinach and cheese mixture into pan and fold overhanging dough over filling. Brush with oil, then layer remaining 4 sheets of phyllo dough, brushing each with oil. Tuck overhanging dough into pan to seal filling.

Bake in preheated oven for 30 to 40 minutes, until golden brown. Cut into squares and serve while hot.

Greek Honey Cake

Ingredients

1 cup all-purpose flour
1 1/2 teaspoons baking powder
1/4 teaspoon salt
1/2 teaspoon ground cinnamon
1 teaspoon orange zest
3/4 cup butter
3/4 cup white sugar
3 eggs
1/4 cup milk
1 cup chopped walnuts

1 cup white sugar
1 cup honey
3/4 cup water
1 teaspoon lemon juice

Directions

Preheat oven to 350 degrees F (175 degrees C). Grease and flour a 9 inch square pan. Combine the flour, baking powder, salt, cinnamon and orange rind. Set aside.

In a large bowl, cream together the butter and 3/4 cup sugar until light and fluffy. Beat in the eggs one at a time. Beat in the flour mixture alternately with the milk, mixing just until incorporated. Stir in the walnuts.

Pour batter into prepared pan. Bake in the preheated oven for 40 minutes, or until a toothpick inserted into the center of the cake comes out clean. Allow to cool for 15 minutes, then cut into diamond shapes. Pour honey syrup over the cake.

For the Honey Syrup: In a saucepan, combine honey, 1 cup sugar and water. Bring to a simmer and cook 5 minutes. Stir in lemon juice, bring to a boil and cook for 2 minutes.

Sofrito (Greek Lamb Recipe)

Ingredients

2 tablespoons all-purpose flour
1 pound boneless lamb meat, cut into bite-sized pieces
1 teaspoon salt
1 teaspoon pepper
2 tablespoons olive oil
4 cloves garlic, peeled and minced
1 bunch fresh parsley, chopped
1 cup red wine vinegar

Directions

Place flour in a medium bowl. Season lamb with salt and pepper, and dredge in flour to evenly coat.

Heat olive oil in a medium skillet over medium heat, and cook the lamb until evenly browned. Scrape up the brown bits from the surface of the skillet. Mix in garlic, parsley, and red wine vinegar. Reduce heat, cover, and simmer approximately 30 minutes, stirring occasionally.

Octapodi Kokkinisto (Greek Octopus in Tomato

ngredients

 pounds octopus, cut into 3-inch
ieces
/4 cup olive oil
 small red onions, cut into thin
vedges
 bay leaves
 cups crushed tomatoes
/2 teaspoon sea salt
reshly ground black pepper to
aste

Directions

Place the octopus pieces into a large saucepan. Cover, and cook over medium-high heat until the octopus has released its juices, 10 to 15 minutes. Uncover, and continue simmering until the liquid has reduced to 3 to 4 tablespoons, 20 to 25 minutes.

Drizzle the octopus with olive oil, then stir in the onions and bay leaves. Cook and stir until the onions have softened, about 10 minutes. Add the tomatoes, salt, and pepper. Reduce heat to medium-low, cover, and simmer until the octopus is tender and the sauce has thickened, about 25 minutes. Cook uncovered for the last 10 minutes if the sauce is too thin.

Greek Avocado Relish with Grilled Lamb Kebabs

Ingredients

2 tablespoons olive oil
5 tablespoons lemon juice, divided
2 cloves garlic, finely chopped
1/2 teaspoon salt
1/4 teaspoon black pepper, freshly ground
1 1/2 pounds leg of lamb, trimmed and cut into 1 1/2-inch cubes
1/3 cup English or hothouse cucumber, diced
1/4 cup Kalamata olives, pitted and finely chopped
3 tablespoons red onion, finely chopped
1 tablespoon fresh oregano, chopped
1 large firm-ripe Chilean Hass avocado, halved, pitted and peeled, cut into 1/4-inch pieces

Directions

In sealable plastic bag, combine olive oil, 2 tablespoons of the lemon juice, garlic, salt and pepper. Add lamb. Seal bag and turn to coat lamb completely. Refrigerate 1 hour.

For relish, in small bowl stir together cucumbers, olives, onion, the remaining 3 tablespoons lemon juice and oregano. Stir to mix. Gently stir in avocado pieces. Cover tightly by placing plastic wrap directly on the surface of the relish.

Remove lamb cubes from marinade and thread 4 cubes onto each of 8 skewers. Grill or broil about 4 minutes per side, or until desired degree of doneness. Serve kabobs with relish.

Sheila's Greek Style Avocado Dip

Ingredients

1 avocado - peeled, pitted and diced
1 clove garlic, minced
2 tablespoons lime juice
1 roma (plum) tomato, seeded and diced
1/4 cup crumbled feta cheese

Directions

Mash together the avocado, garlic, and lime juice in a bowl until nearly smooth. Fold in the diced tomato and feta cheese.

Oven Roasted Greek Potatoes

Ingredients

2 teaspoons lemon pepper
1/2 teaspoon dried marjoram
1 teaspoon dried basil
1/8 teaspoon dried thyme
1 teaspoon dried rosemary
1/4 cup white wine
1 cup water
2 tablespoons olive oil
2 tablespoons Italian salad dressing
2 cloves garlic, minced
1 lemon, juiced
1 tablespoon lemon zest
6 medium potatoes, peeled and quartered

Directions

In a small bowl, mix the lemon pepper, marjoram, basil, thyme, and rosemary. In a separate bowl, mix the wine, water, olive oil, dressing, garlic, lemon juice, lemon zest, and 1/2 the seasoning mixture. Pour into a medium glass baking dish. Place potatoes in the dish, coat with the mixture, and sprinkle with remaining seasonings. Cover, and refrigerate 8 hours, or overnight.

Preheat oven to 350 degrees F (175 degrees C).

Bake potatoes 1 hour and 15 minutes in the preheated oven, basting once half way through the bake time.

Easy Greek Skillet Dinner

Ingredients

1/2 pound dried elbow macaroni
1 pound lean ground beef
2 cloves garlic, pressed or minced
2 medium carrots, quartered lengthwise and sliced
1 large zucchini, quartered lengthwise and sliced
1 1/2 tablespoons dried oregano leaves
salt and pepper
1 (10.75 ounce) can condensed tomato soup, plus
1 (10.75 ounce) can water
crumbled feta cheese (optional)

Directions

Bring a large pot of lightly salted water to a boil. Cook elbow macaroni for 8 to 10 minutes or until al dente; drain, and set aside.

Brown ground beef with garlic in a large skillet over medium heat. Strain off fat, if necessary. When meat is lightly browned, add carrots and cook until tender, about 5 minutes. Stir in zucchini and oregano, and continue cooking another 5 minutes. Season to taste with salt and pepper.

When vegetables are tender, stir in tomato soup, water, and prepared elbow macaroni, and cook for another 5 to 10 minutes. Serve with crumbled feta cheese on top, if desired.

Fran's Greek Butter Cookies

Ingredients

2 cups sifted all-purpose flour
1 cup butter
4 tablespoons confectioners' sugar
1 cup chopped walnuts
2 tablespoons water
2 teaspoons vanilla extract
1/3 cup confectioners' sugar for decoration
30 whole cloves

Directions

Cream butter, add sugar gradually cream until smooth. Blend in flour. Stir in nuts, water, and vanilla. Mix well.

Shape into small 1 inch balls, press down while pressing in 1 whole clove on ungreased baking sheet.

Bake at 350 degrees F (175 degrees C) for 20 minutes. While still warm roll into confectioners' sugar. If desired roll again when cooled.

ngredients

1/2 pounds potatoes, peeled
nd cubed
/3 cup olive oil
cloves garlic, minced
/4 cup whole, pitted kalamata
lives
1/3 cups chopped tomatoes
teaspoon dried oregano
alt and pepper to taste

Directions

In a large saute pan, heat the oil over medium heat. Add the potatoes and stir. Stir in the garlic. Add the olives and cook and stir for several minutes. Stir in the tomatoes, and oregano.

Reduce heat, cover and simmer for 30 minutes or until potatoes are tender. Season to taste with salt and pepper.

Greek-Style Baked Salmon

Ingredients

8 (5 ounce) salmon fillets, with skin
1/4 cup olive oil
4 plum tomatoes, diced
1/2 cup crumbled feta cheese
1/4 red onion, diced
1 tablespoon chopped fresh basil
4 kalamata olives, sliced
1 tablespoon lemon juice

Directions

Preheat an oven to 350 degrees F (175 degrees C).

Brush each salmon fillet on all sides with olive oil and arrange into the bottom of a glass baking dish with the skin side facing down. Scatter the tomatoes, feta cheese, onion, basil, and olives over the fillets; sprinkle with the lemon juice.

Bake in the preheated oven until the salmon flakes easily with a fork, about 20 minutes.

Greek Lamb Kabobs with Yogurt-Mint Salsa Verde

Ingredients

Lamb Skewers:
8 6-inch rosemary sprigs
1 tablespoon minced garlic
1 tablespoon chopped fresh thyme
1/3 cup extra virgin olive oil
1/4 cup sherry vinegar
1 teaspoon sea salt
1 teaspoon ground white pepper
1 1/2 pounds lamb tenderloin, cut into 2-inch pieces

Salsa Verde:
1/4 cup fresh lemon juice 1/2
cup extra virgin olive oil 1/3
cup Greek yogurt
1 crushed garlic clove
1/4 teaspoon sea salt
2 teaspoons chopped fresh mint
1 teaspoon chopped fresh oregano
1 teaspoon chopped fresh parsley
1 teaspoon small capers
1 anchovy filet

Directions

Soak the rosemary skewers in water for 30 minutes. Meanwhile, whisk together the garlic, thyme, olive oil, sherry vinegar, salt, and pepper in a glass bowl. Toss the lamb pieces in the marinade, and allow to marinate at room temperature for 30 minutes. After the lamb has marinated, thread onto the rosemary sprigs.

While the lamb is marinating, prepare the salsa verde by placing the lemon juice, olive oil, yogurt, garlic, salt, mint, oregano, parsley, capers, and anchovy filet into the bowl of a blender. Blend until smooth, then pour into a serving dish and set aside.

Preheat an outdoor grill for medium heat.

Cook the lamb skewers, turning occasionally, until no longer pink, about 8 minutes. Serve with salsa verde.

Briam (Greek Mixed Vegetables in Tomato Sauce)

Ingredients

4 tomatoes
1/2 cup olive oil
2 tablespoons red wine vinegar
2 tablespoons white sugar
1/3 cup chopped fresh parsley
1/3 cup chopped fresh mint
1/3 cup chopped fresh basil
2 tablespoons fresh oregano
1/4 cup capers
2 cloves garlic
salt and ground black pepper to taste

2 tablespoons olive oil
2 onions, sliced
2 potatoes, sliced
2 eggplant, sliced
3 zucchini, sliced
3 green bell peppers, sliced
2 cups okra

Directions

Preheat oven to 350 degrees F (175 degrees C). Place three of the tomatoes, the 1/2 cup olive oil, red wine vinegar, sugar, parsley, mint, basil, oregano, capers, and garlic in the bowl of a food processor and process to create a fresh tomato sauce. Season with salt and black pepper; set aside. Chop the remaining tomato; set aside.

Heat the 2 tablespoons olive oil in a skillet over medium heat, and cook and stir the onions until slightly golden, about 10 minutes.

Stir together the onions, potatoes, eggplant, zucchini, bell peppers, okra, the reserved chopped tomato, and the fresh tomato sauce, and place the mixture in a large baking pan. If needed, stir in a little water so that the vegetables are just covered with sauce.

Bake in the preheated oven until all vegetables are tender, about 1 hour.

Ingredients

1/3 cup crumbled feta cheese
1/3 cup grated Parmesan cheese
1 (8 ounce) package cream cheese, softened
1 tablespoon sun-dried tomato pesto

Directions

Blend the feta cheese, Parmesan cheese, cream cheese, and sun-dried tomato pesto in a food processor until completely mixed. Serve immediately or chill overnight.

Greek Olive and Onion Bread

Ingredients

2 (.25 ounce) packages rapid rise yeast
1/2 cup warm water
2 tablespoons extra-virgin olive oil
2 large red onions, diced
7 cups bread flour
1 1/2 teaspoons salt
1/2 teaspoon white sugar
1/4 cup chopped fresh dill
1/4 teaspoon garlic powder (optional)
2 cups pitted kalamata olives, chopped
1 3/4 cups warm water

Directions

Sprinkle the yeast over 1/2 cup of warm water in a small bowl. The water should be no more than 100 degrees F (40 degrees C). Let stand for 5 minutes until the yeast softens and begins to form a creamy foam.

Heat a large skillet over medium heat and add the olive oil and the onions. Cook and stir for 3 minutes, or until onions are soft. Remove the onions from heat and reserve.

Combine the bread flour, salt, sugar, dill, garlic powder, olives, and cooked onions in a large bowl and mix well. Add the yeast mixture and the remaining 1 3/4 cup water. Mix well until the ingredients have pulled together and have formed a sticky dough. Turn the dough out onto a lightly floured surface and knead until smooth and elastic, about 8 minutes.

Lightly oil a large bowl, then place the dough in the bowl and turn to coat with oil. Cover with a light cloth and let rise in a warm place (80 to 95 degrees F (27 to 35 degrees C)) until doubled in volume, about 1 hour.

Lightly grease two baking sheets. Deflate the risen dough and turn it out onto a lightly floured surface. Use a knife to divide the dough into two equal pieces-don't tear it. Shape into dough into round loaves, and place the loaves into the prepared pans. Cover the loaves with a damp cloth and let rise until doubled in volume, about 40 minutes.

Preheat an oven to 450 degrees F (230 degrees C).

Bake loaves in the preheated oven until the tops are golden brown and the bottoms sound hollow when tapped, about 40 minutes. Cool slightly before slicing.

Greek-Style Green Beans

Ingredients

2 cups fresh green beans (2-inch pieces)
1/2 small sweet onion, cut into thin wedges
1 tablespoon olive oil
1 small tomato, cut into eighths
1/2 teaspoon dried oregano
1/4 teaspoon salt
Dash pepper

Directions

Place the beans in a saucepan and cover with water; bring to a boil. Cook for 3-4 minutes or until crisp-tender; drain.

In a small skillet, saute onion in oil for 3 minutes. Add the beans; saute for 5 minutes or until tender. Reduce heat. Add the tomato, oregano, salt and pepper; cool 1 minutes longer or until heated through.

Greek Spaghetti

Ingredients

1 (16 ounce) package spaghetti, broken into 2-inch pieces
4 cups cooked, cubed chicken breast
2 (10 ounce) packages frozen chopped spinach, thawed and squeezed dry
2 (10.75 ounce) cans condensed cream of chicken soup, undiluted
1 cup mayonnaise
1 cup sour cream
3 celery ribs, chopped
1 small onion, chopped
1/2 cup chopped green pepper
1 (2 ounce) jar diced pimientos, drained
1/2 teaspoon lemon-pepper seasoning
1 cup shredded Monterey Jack cheese
1/2 cup soft bread crumbs
1/2 cup shredded Parmesan cheese

Directions

Cook spaghetti according to package directions; drain. Return spaghetti to saucepan. Stir in the chicken, spinach, soup, mayonnaise, sour cream, celery, onion, green pepper, pimientos and lemon-pepper.

Transfer to a greased 13-in. x 9-in. x 2-in. baking dish (dish will be full). Top with Monterey Jack cheese, bread crumbs and Parmesan cheese. Bake, uncovered, at 350 degrees F for 25-30 minutes or until heated through.

Greek Salad V

Ingredients

1 English cucumber, diced
2 large tomatoes, each cut into 8 wedges
1/2 cup thinly sliced red onion
1/2 cup thinly sliced green bell pepper
1/2 cup whole, pitted kalamata olives
1 cup crumbled feta cheese
2 tablespoons dried oregano
2 teaspoons fresh lemon juice
2 tablespoons olive oil
salt and pepper to taste

Directions

In a medium bowl, layer cucumbers, tomatoes, onion, bell pepper, kalamata olives, and feta cheese. Sprinkle with oregano, then drizzle with lemon juice and olive oil. Season with salt and pepper to taste.

Greek Pork Cutlets

Ingredients

1 (1 pound) pork tenderloin
1 small onion, chopped
2 tablespoons lemon juice
1 tablespoon minced fresh parsley
2 garlic cloves, minced
3/4 teaspoon dried thyme
1/8 teaspoon pepper
CUCUMBER SAUCE:
1 small tomato, seeded and chopped
2/3 cup reduced-fat plain yogurt
1/2 cup chopped seeded cucumber
1 tablespoon finely chopped onion
1/2 teaspoon lemon juice
1/8 teaspoon garlic powder

Directions

Cut pork into eight slices; flatten to 1/2-in. thickness. In a large resealable plastic bag, combine the onion, lemon juice, parsley, garlic, thyme and pepper; add pork. Seal bag and turn to coat; refrigerate for 4 hours or overnight. In a small bowl, combine the cucumber sauce ingredients. Cover and refrigerate until serving.

Drain pork and discard marinade. Place on a broiler pan coated with nonstick cooking spray. Broil 4 in. from the heat for 6-8 minutes on each side or until juices run clear. Serve with cucumber sauce.

ngredients

4 MissionB® 98% Fat Free Burrito
Size Flour Tortillas
4 boneless, skinless chicken
breasts
1/2 cup fat-free Italian dressing
1/2 cup diced tomatoes
1 (4 ounce) can chopped black
olives, drained
1/2 cup peeled and seeded
cucumber, chopped
1 tablespoon fresh lemon juice

1/2 cup fat free sour cream mixed
with:
1 1/2 teaspoons crushed garlic
1/2 teaspoon onion powder

2 cups assorted greens

Directions

Marinate chicken in dressing 2 hours to overnight.

Combine tomatoes, olives, cucumber, lemon juice, and 1/2 cup of the sour cream mixture. Reserve.

Grill chicken, let cool, and cut into very thin strips.

Spread each tortilla with 1 tablespoon sour cream mixture.

Lay one quarter of chicken strips on tortilla, top with 1/2 cup of vegetable mixture and 1/2 cup of salad greens.

Fold in sides of tortilla and roll up tightly. Cut on a diagonal and serve.

Marinated Greek Chicken Kabobs

Ingredients

1 (8 ounce) container fat-free plain yogurt
1/3 cup crumbled feta cheese with basil and sun-dried tomatoes
1/2 teaspoon lemon zest
2 tablespoons fresh lemon juice
2 teaspoons dried oregano
1/2 teaspoon salt
1/4 teaspoon ground black pepper
1/4 teaspoon crushed dried rosemary
1 pound skinless, boneless chicken breast halves - cut into 1 inch pieces
1 large red onion, cut into wedges
1 large green bell pepper, cut into 1 1/2 inch pieces

Directions

In a large shallow baking dish, mix the yogurt, feta cheese, lemon zest, lemon juice, oregano, salt, pepper, and rosemary. Place the chicken in the dish, and turn to coat. Cover, and marinate 3 hours in the refrigerator.

Preheat an outdoor grill for high heat.

Thread the chicken, onion wedges, and green bell pepper pieces alternately onto skewers. Discard remaining yogurt mixture.

Grill skewers on the prepared grill until the chicken is no longer pink and juices run clear.

Greek Lemon Chicken Soup

Ingredients

3 cups chicken broth
1/2 cup fresh lemon juice
1/2 cup shredded carrots
1/2 cup chopped onion
1/2 cup chopped celery
3 tablespoons chicken soup base
1/4 teaspoon ground white pepper
1/4 cup margarine
1/4 cup all-purpose flour
1 cup cooked white rice
1 cup diced, cooked chicken meat
16 slices lemon
3 egg yolks

Directions

In a large pot, combine the chicken broth, lemon juice, carrots, onions, celery, soup base, and white pepper. Bring to a boil on high, then simmer for 20 minutes.

Blend the butter and the flour together. Then gradually add it to the soup mixture. Simmer for 10 minutes more, stirring frequently.

Meanwhile, beat the egg yolks until light in color. Gradually add some of the hot soup to the egg yolks, stirring constantly. Return the egg mixture to the soup pot and heat through. Add the rice and chicken. Ladle hot soup into bowls and garnish with lemon slices.

Easy Greek Yogurt Cucumber Sauce

Ingredients

1 cup plain yogurt
1 cup sour cream
1 teaspoon white vinegar
1/2 teaspoon lemon juice
1 small cucumber - peeled, seeded, and finely chopped
1 green onion
1 garlic clove, minced
1/4 cup crumbled feta cheese
1/2 teaspoon oregano
1/4 teaspoon lemon zest
salt and pepper to taste

Directions

Stir together the yogurt, sour cream, vinegar, lemon juice, cucumber, green onion, garlic, feta cheese, oregano, lemon zest, salt, and pepper in a bowl; cover and chill 8 hours or overnight before serving.

Greek Tomatoes

Ingredients

4 medium tomatoes, cut into 1/4 inch slices
1 small red onion, thinly sliced and separated into rings
3/4 cup crumbled feta cheese
1/4 cup minced fresh parsley
1/2 teaspoon salt
1/2 teaspoon coarsely ground pepper
1 tablespoon olive or canola oil

Directions

Arrange tomato and onion slices on a plate. Sprinkle with the feta cheese, parsley, salt and pepper. Drizzle with oil. Cover and refrigerate for 15 minutes.

Warm Greek Pita Sandwiches With Turkey and

Ingredients

1/2 cup sour cream
1/2 cup plain low-fat yogurt
1/2 cup cucumber, peeled, grated and squeezed as dry as possible
2 teaspoons red or rice wine vinegar
2 garlic cloves, minced
1/2 teaspoon Salt and pepper, to taste
4 large pitas
2 tablespoons olive oil
1 large onion, peeled, halved and cut into chunky wedges
3 cups leftover roast turkey, pulled into bite-sized pieces
1 teaspoon oregano
1 1/2 cups shredded lettuce (preferably romaine)
1 cup cherry tomatoes, halved and lightly salted

Directions

Adjust oven rack to middle position. Heat oven to 300 degrees.

In a small bowl, mix sour cream, yogurt, cucumber, vinegar, 1 minced garlic clove, and salt and pepper to taste; set aside.

Place pitas in oven; bake until warm and pliable, 7 minutes. Cut in half. Meanwhile, heat oil in a large skillet over high heat. Carefully add onion; saute until spotty brown but still crisp, 2 to 3 minutes. Add turkey, oregano and remaining minced garlic; continue to saute until heated through, another 2 minutes.

Serve, letting guests fill their own pitas with lettuce first, followed by turkey, tomatoes and cucumber sauce.

Ingredients

1 cup uncooked long grain brown rice
2 1/2 cups water
1 avocado - peeled, pitted, and diced
1/4 cup lemon juice
2 vine-ripened tomatoes, diced
1 1/2 cups diced English cucumbers
1/3 cup diced red onion
1/2 cup crumbled feta cheese
1/4 cup sliced Kalamata olives
1/4 cup chopped fresh mint
3 tablespoons olive oil
1 teaspoon lemon zest
1/2 teaspoon minced garlic
1/2 teaspoon kosher salt
1/2 teaspoon ground black pepper

Directions

Bring the brown rice and water to a boil in a saucepan over high heat. Reduce the heat to medium-low, cover, and simmer until the rice is tender and the liquid has been absorbed, 45 to 50 minutes; remove from heat and allow to cool, fluffing occasionally with a fork.

Toss the avocado and lemon juice together in a large bowl. Add the tomatoes, cucumber, onion, feta, olives, mint, olive oil, lemon zest, garlic, salt, and pepper to the bowl; lightly toss the mixture until evenly combined. Fold the cooled rice gently into the mixture. Serve immediately or chill up to 1 hour; the salad does not last well for more than a day as the tomato and cucumber begin to release their juices and the salad becomes watery.

Party-Size Greek Couscous Salad

Ingredients

3 (6 ounce) packages garlic and herb couscous mix (or any flavor you prefer)
1 pint cherry tomatoes, cut in half
1 (5 ounce) jar pitted kalamata olives, halved
1 cup mixed bell peppers (green, red, yellow, orange), diced
1 cucumber, sliced and then halved
1/2 cup parsley, finely chopped
1 (8 ounce) package crumbled feta cheese
1/2 cup Greek vinaigrette salad dressing

Directions

Cook couscous according to package directions. Transfer to a large serving bowl to cool. Stir to break up clusters of couscous.

When the couscous has cooled to room temperature, mix in tomatoes, olives, bell peppers, cucumber, parsley, and feta. Gradually stir vinaigrette into couscous until you arrive at desired moistness.

Greek Souzoukaklia

Ingredients

1 1/2 pounds ground beef
1 onion, chopped
3/8 cup raisins, chopped
1 1/2 teaspoons chopped flat leaf parsley
1/2 teaspoon cayenne pepper
1/2 teaspoon ground cinnamon
1/2 teaspoon ground coriander
1 pinch ground nutmeg
1/2 teaspoon white sugar
salt and pepper to taste
skewers
1 tablespoon vegetable oil

Directions

Preheat grill for high heat.

In a large bowl, mix together ground beef, onion, raisins, and parsley. Season with cayenne pepper, cinnamon, coriander, nutmeg, sugar, salt, and pepper, and mix well. Form into 6 flat sausages around skewers. Lightly brush sausages with oil; this prevents sticking to the grill.

Arrange skewers on hot grill grate. Cook for approximately 15 minutes, turning occasionally to brown evenly, until well done.

Greek Pasta with Tomatoes and White Beans

Ingredients

2 (14.5 ounce) cans Italian-style diced tomatoes
1 (19 ounce) can cannellini beans, drained and rinsed
10 ounces fresh spinach, washed and chopped
8 ounces penne pasta
1/2 cup crumbled feta cheese

Directions

Cook the pasta in a large pot of boiling salted water until al dente.

Meanwhile, combine tomatoes and beans in a large non-stick skillet. Bring to a boil over medium high heat. Reduce heat, and simmer 10 minutes.

Add spinach to the sauce; cook for 2 minutes or until spinach wilts, stirring constantly.

Serve sauce over pasta, and sprinkle with feta.

Oia Greek Salad

Ingredients

1 English cucumber, diced
2 pints grape tomatoes, halved
1 (4 ounce) container crumbled feta cheese
1 (4 ounce) jar capers, drained
1/2 cup diced red onion
1/4 cup Greek salad dressing, such as Yazzo!
1/2 cup Greek olives, drained

Directions

Keep all of the ingredients separate until ready to serve so the onion doesn't overpower everything. To prepare the salad, toss the cucumber, tomatoes, feta cheese, capers, onion, and salad dressing together in a large bowl until evenly coated. Sprinkle with the Greek olives to serve.

Taramousalata (Greek Caviar Spread)

Ingredients

1 potato
8 slices white sandwich bread
2 cups milk
1/2 cup carp roe
1 small onion, chopped
1/4 cup fresh lemon juice
1/2 cup olive oil, or more if needed
2 Greek olives (optional)

Directions

Preheat an oven to 450 degrees F (230 degrees C). Prick the potato in several places with a fork and place on a baking sheet.

Bake the potato in the preheated oven easily pierced with a fork, 50 minutes to 1 hour. Cool completely in refrigerator. Peel and chop.

Place the bread slices in a shallow dish; pour the milk over the bread to cover completely. Allow to soak a few minutes before squeezing as much moisture as possible from the bread, discarding the milk.

Blend the bread, potato, carp roe, onion, lemon juice, and olive oil together in a food processor until fluffy, about 1 minute. Add more olive oil if needed to reach a desired consistency; chill. Garnish with the Greek olives to serve.

Greek Pasta and Beef

Ingredients

1 (16 ounce) package elbow macaroni
1 pound ground beef
1 large onion, chopped
1 garlic clove, minced
1 (8 ounce) can tomato sauce
1/2 cup water
1 teaspoon salt
1/2 teaspoon ground cinnamon
1/4 teaspoon ground nutmeg 1/4 teaspoon pepper
1 egg, lightly beaten
1/2 cup grated Parmesan cheese
SAUCE:
1 cup butter
1/4 cup all-purpose flour
1/4 teaspoon ground cinnamon
3 cups milk
2 eggs, lightly beaten
1/3 cup grated Parmesan cheese

Directions

Cook macaroni according to package directions. In a large skillet, cook beef, onion and garlic over medium heat until meat is no longer pink; drain. Stir in the tomato sauce, water and seasonings. Cover and simmer for 10 minutes, stirring occasionally. Drain macaroni.

In a large bowl, combine the macaroni, egg and Parmesan cheese; set aside. For sauce, in a large saucepan, melt butter; stir in flour and cinnamon until smooth. Gradually add milk. Bring to a boil over medium heat; cook and stir for 2 minutes or until slightly thickened. Remove from the heat. Stir a small amount to hot mixture into eggs; return all to pan, stirring constantly. Stir in cheese.

In a greased 3-qt. baking dish, spread half of the macaroni mixture. Top with beef mixture and remaining macaroni mixture. Pour sauce over the top. Bake, uncovered, at 350 degrees F for 45-50 minutes or until bubbly and heated through. Let stand for 5 minutes before serving.

Greek Garlic-Lemon Potatoes

Ingredients

3 pounds potatoes, peeled and cubed
3 cups hot water
1/2 cup fresh lemon juice
1/3 cup vegetable oil
1 tablespoon olive oil
1 1/2 teaspoons dried oregano
2 teaspoons salt
1/2 teaspoon ground black pepper
2 cloves garlic, minced
1/4 cup chopped fresh parsley

Directions

Preheat oven to 475 degrees F (245 degrees C).

Place the cubed potatoes, water, lemon juice, vegetable oil, and olive oil in a 12x18 inch baking dish or roasting pan. Season with oregano, salt, pepper, and garlic.

Roast, uncovered, in the preheated oven until the potatoes are tender and golden brown and the water has evaporated, about 1 1/2 hours. Stir the potatoes every 20 minutes as they bake, adding more water as necessary to prevent sticking. Allow the water to evaporate during the final 15 to 20 minutes of cooking, but be careful that the potatoes do not burn. Stir in the chopped fresh parsley, and serve.

Greek Veggie Salad II

Ingredients

1 large cucumber, chopped
2 roma (plum) tomatoes, chopped
1 (5 ounce) jar pitted kalamata
olives
1 (4 ounce) package feta cheese,
crumbled
1 red onion, halved and thinly
sliced
1/2 (10 ounce) package baby
greens
1/2 (10 ounce) package romaine
lettuce leaves

6 tablespoons olive oil
1 teaspoon garlic powder
1 teaspoon dried oregano
1 teaspoon dried basil
1 teaspoon Dijon mustard
1 teaspoon lemon juice
1 1/2 cups red wine vinegar

Directions

In a large bowl, mix the cucumber, tomatoes, olives, feta cheese, red onion, baby greens, and romaine. In a separate bowl, mix the olive oil, garlic powder, oregano, basil, mustard, lemon juice, and red wine vinegar. Pour dressing over the vegetables, and toss to coat.

Vaselopita - Greek New Years Cake

Ingredients

1 cup butter
2 cups white sugar
3 cups all-purpose flour
6 eggs
2 teaspoons baking powder
1 cup warm milk (110 degrees F/45 degrees C)
1/2 teaspoon baking soda
1 tablespoon fresh lemon juice
1/4 cup blanched slivered almonds
2 tablespoons white sugar

Directions

Preheat oven to 350 degrees F (175 degrees C). Generously grease a 10 inch round cake pan.

In a medium bowl, cream the butter and sugar together until light. Stir in the flour and mix until the mixture is mealy. Add the eggs one at a time, mixing well after each addition. Combine the baking powder and milk, add to the egg mixture, mix well. Then combine the lemon juice and baking soda, stir into the batter. Pour into the prepared cake pan.

Bake for 20 minutes in the preheated oven. Remove and sprinkle the nuts and sugar over the cake, then return it to the oven for 20 to 30 additional minutes, until cake springs back to the touch. Gently cut a small hole in the cake and place a quarter in the hole. Try to cover the hole with sugar. Cool cake on a rack for 10 minutes before inverting onto a plate.

Serve cake warm. Each person in the family gets a slice starting with the youngest. The person who gets the quarter in their piece, gets good luck for the whole year!

Greek Orzo Salad

Ingredients

1 1/2 cups uncooked orzo pasta
2 (6 ounce) cans marinated
artichoke hearts
1 tomato, seeded and chopped
1 cucumber, seeded and chopped
1 red onion, chopped
1 cup crumbled feta cheese
1 (2 ounce) can black olives,
drained
1/4 cup chopped fresh parsley
1 tablespoon lemon juice
1/2 teaspoon dried oregano
1/2 teaspoon lemon pepper

Directions

Bring a large pot of lightly salted water to a boil. Add pasta and cook for 8 to 10 minutes or until al dente; drain. Drain artichoke hearts, reserving liquid.

In large bowl combine pasta, artichoke hearts, tomato, cucumber, onion, feta, olives, parsley, lemon juice, oregano and lemon pepper. Toss and chill for 1 hour in refrigerator.

Just before serving, drizzle reserved artichoke marinade over salad.

Ingredients

1 1/3 pounds ground beef
1 tablespoon plain yogurt
2 teaspoons dried thyme
salt and pepper to taste
4 ounces feta cheese

Directions

Preheat grill for indirect heat.

In a large bowl, mix together ground beef, yogurt, thyme, and salt and pepper. Form meat into 8 patties, about 2 to 3 inches in diameter.

Cut the cheese into 4 slices. Place one cheese slice between two patties, and seal the edges. Repeat with remaining beef patties and cheese slices. Set bifteki aside.

Brush grate with oil, and arrange bifteki on hot grate. Cover, and cook for 15 to 20 minutes, or until meat is cooked through and cheese is melted.

Greek Orange Roast Lamb

ngredients

large orange, juiced
tablespoons dark French mustard
tablespoons olive oil
teaspoons dried oregano
alt and pepper to taste
0 potatoes, peeled and cut into
-inch pieces
(3 pound) half leg of lamb, bone-
n
cloves garlic

Directions

Preheat oven to 375 degrees F (190 degrees C).

In large bowl, whisk together the orange juice, mustard, olive oil, oregano, salt, and pepper. Stir the potatoes into the bowl to coat with orange juice mixture. Remove potatoes with a slotted spoon, and place them into a large roasting pan.

Cut slits into the lamb meat, and stuff the garlic cloves into the slits. Rub remaining orange juice mixture from bowl all over the lamb, and place the lamb on top of the potatoes in the roasting pan. If there's any remaining orange juice mixture, pour it over the lamb.

Roast in the preheated oven until the potatoes are tender and the lamb is cooked to medium, about 1 hour. A meat thermometer inserted into the thickest part of the meat should read 140 degrees F (60 degrees C). Check every 20 to 30 minutes while roasting, and add a bit of hot water if you find the potatoes are drying out. If the lamb finishes cooking before the potatoes, remove the lamb to a cutting board or serving platter and cover with foil while the potatoes continue to bake in the oven.

A Lot More Than Plain Spinach Pie (Greek

Ingredients

3 eggs
1 pound chopped fresh spinach
3 leeks, chopped
5 green onions, chopped
2 1/3 cups crumbled feta cheese
1 bunch parsley, chopped
1 bunch dill, chopped
1 bunch spearmint, chopped
1 teaspoon white sugar
1 cup milk
3/4 cup olive oil
1 pinch salt and ground black pepper to taste

2 1/2 cups all-purpose flour
1/2 cup semolina flour
1 pinch salt
1/4 cup olive oil
2 cups water

1 1/4 cups grated Parmesan cheese (optional)
2 tablespoons cold butter, cut into pieces
2 tablespoons olive oil

Directions

Preheat an oven to 350 degrees F (175 degrees C). Grease a deep 9x9 inch baking dish.

Beat the eggs in a mixing bowl, then stir in the spinach, leeks, green onions, feta cheese, parsley, dill, spearmint, sugar, milk, and 3/4 cup of olive oil until evenly mixed. Season to taste with salt and pepper; set aside. Whisk together the all-purpose flour, semolina flour, and 1 pinch of salt in a mixing bowl. Stir in 1/4 cup of olive oil and the water until no lumps remain. Pour 2/3 of the batter into the prepared 9x9 inch pan, and spread out evenly. Spoon the spinach filling over the batter, then spoon the remaining batter overtop. Sprinkle with the Parmesan cheese, butter pieces, and 2 tablespoons of olive oil.

Bake in the preheated oven until the bottom crust and top has firmed and nicely browned, about 1 hour.

Standard Greek Salad

Ingredients

5 cucumbers, sliced
5 large tomatoes, coarsely
chopped
1/2 red onion, chopped
1 (4 ounce) package feta cheese,
crumbled
1 (2.25 ounce) can pitted green
olives, chopped
1/4 cup red wine vinegar

Directions

In a large bowl, toss together cucumbers, tomatoes, red onion, feta cheese, and green olives. Sprinkle with red wine vinegar. Refrigerate until serving.

Mediterranean Greek Salad

Ingredients

3 cucumbers, seeded and sliced
1 1/2 cups crumbled feta cheese
1 cup black olives, pitted and sliced
3 cups diced roma tomatoes
1/3 cup diced oil packed sun-dried tomatoes, drained, oil reserved
1/2 red onion, sliced

Directions

In a large salad bowl, toss together the cucumbers, feta cheese, olives, roma tomatoes, sun-dried tomatoes, 2 tablespoons reserved sun-dried tomato oil, and red onion. Chill until serving.

Greek Burgers

Ingredients

1 cup mayonnaise
2 teaspoons minced garlic
2 pounds ground lamb
1/4 cup bread crumbs
1 bulb fennel, chopped
3 tablespoons shallots, minced
1 teaspoon dried oregano
1/2 teaspoon salt
ground black pepper to taste
8 hamburger buns

Directions

In a small bowl, mix together mayonnaise and minced garlic. Cover, and refrigerate for at least 2 hours.

Preheat grill for high heat.

Mix together lamb, bread crumbs, fennel, shallot, oregano, and salt. Form into 3/4 inch thick patties, and sprinkle black pepper over surfaces.

Brush grate with oil, and place burgers on grill. Cook for 3 to 5 minutes per side, turning once, or until done. Serve on buns with garlic mayonnaise.

SwansonB® Greek-Style Beef Stew

Ingredients

2 pounds boneless beef bottom round roast or chuck pot roast, cut into 1-inch pieces
1 (16 ounce) bag frozen whole small white onions
1 (16 ounce) package fresh or frozen whole baby carrots
2 tablespoons all-purpose flour
1 3/4 cups SwansonB® Beef Broth (Regular, 50% Less Sodium or Certified Organic)
1 (5.5 ounce) can Campbell'sB® V8B® 100% Vegetable Juice
1 tablespoon packed brown sugar
Bouquet Garni
Hot cooked egg noodles

Directions

Place the beef, onions and carrots into a 3 1/2- to 6-quart slow cooker. Sprinkle with the flour and toss to coat.

Stir the broth, vegetable juice and brown sugar in a medium bowl. Pour the broth mixture over the beef and vegetables. Submerge the Bouquet Garni into the broth mixture.

Cover and cook on LOW for 8 to 9 hours* or until the beef is fork-tender. Remove the Bouquet Garni. Serve the beef mixture over the noodles.

Greek Egg Biscuits

Ingredients

2 cups unsalted butter
1 cup white sugar
1 tablespoon vanilla extract
5 eggs
5 1/2 cups all-purpose flour
1/2 teaspoon salt
3 tablespoons baking powder
1/4 cup sesame seeds

Directions

In large mixing bowl, beat butter until light and fluffy. Add the sugar and beat for 10 minutes on medium speed. Add four of the eggs, one at a time, and beat well after each addition. Beat in the vanilla. Combine the flour, baking powder, and salt in a separate bowl. Add to the butter mixture and stir to form soft, cohesive dough. Add flour if dough is too soft to handle easily.

Preheat oven to 350 degrees F. Grease cookie sheets

Lightly flour a work surface. Break off 1 inch lumps of dough and roll on floured surface into ropes about 7 inches long and 1/4 inch in diameter. Cross the ends and twirl dough in a loop in the opposite direction, forming a braid. Place on cookie sheets about 1 inch apart.

Beat remaining egg. Brush onto braids for glaze and sprinkle with sesame seeds. Bake 20 to 25 minutes. Let cool on cookie sheets for 10 minutes, then remove to racks to cool completely.

Greek Spaghetti II

Ingredients

1 pound spaghetti
6 tablespoons butter
1/2 teaspoon salt
1 cup grated Parmesan cheese
1 teaspoon dried oregano

Directions

Preheat oven to 250 degrees F (120 degrees C).

Bring a large pot of lightly salted water to a boil. Add pasta and cook for 8 to 10 minutes or until al dente; drain.

In a medium skillet over medium heat, melt butter with salt and cook until just brown. Remove from heat and toss with pasta, cheese and oregano. Pour into a 7x11 inch baking dish.

Bake in preheated oven 10 to 15 minutes, until hot and bubbly.

Greek Lentil Soup (Fakes)

Ingredients

8 ounces brown lentils
1/4 cup olive oil
1 tablespoon minced garlic
1 onions, minced
1 large carrot, chopped
1 quart water
1 pinch dried oregano
1 pinch crushed dried rosemary
2 bay leaves
1 tablespoon tomato paste
salt and pepper to taste

Directions

Place lentils in a large saucepan, cover with 1 inch of water. Place over medium-high heat and bring to a boil; cook for 10 minutes, then drain lentils into a strainer.

Dry saucepan, pour in olive oil, and place over medium heat. Add garlic, onion, and carrot; cook and stir until the onion has softened and turned translucent, about 5 minutes. Pour in lentils, 1 quart water, oregano, rosemary, and bay leaves. Bring to a boil. Reduce heat to medium-low, cover, and simmer for 10 minutes.

Stir in tomato paste and season to taste with salt and pepper. Cover and simmer until the lentils have softened, 30 to 40 minutes, stirring occasionally. Add additional water if the soup becomes too thick.

Greek Pasta Salad with Roasted Vegetables and

Ingredients

1 red bell pepper, cut into 1/2 inch pieces
1 yellow bell pepper, chopped
1 medium eggplant, cubed
3 small yellow squash, cut in 1/4 inch slices
6 tablespoons extra virgin olive oil
1/4 teaspoon salt
1/4 teaspoon ground black pepper
1 1/2 ounces sun-dried tomatoes, soaked in 1/2 cup boiling water 1/2 cup torn arugula leaves
1/2 cup chopped fresh basil
2 tablespoons balsamic vinegar
2 tablespoons minced garlic
4 ounces crumbled feta cheese
1 (12 ounce) package farfalle pasta

Directions

Preheat oven to 450 degrees F (230 degrees C). Line a cookie sheet with foil, and spray with non-stick cooking spray.

In a medium bowl toss the red bell pepper, yellow bell pepper, eggplant, and squash with 2 tablespoons of the olive oil, salt, and pepper. Arrange on the prepared cookie sheet.

Bake vegetables 25 minutes in the preheated oven, tossing occasionally, until lightly browned.

In a large pot of salted boiling water, cook pasta 10 to 12 minutes, until al dente, and drain.

Drain the softened sun-dried tomatoes and reserve the water. In a large bowl, toss together the roasted vegetables, cooked pasta, sun-drained tomatoes, arugula, and basil. Mix in remaining olive oil, reserved water from tomatoes, balsamic vinegar, garlic, and feta cheese; toss to coat. Season with salt and pepper to taste. Serve immediately, or refrigerate until chilled.

Greek Chicken

Ingredients

4 boneless, skinless chicken breast halves
2 (4 ounce) packages feta or blue cheese
1 (4.5 ounce) can chopped ripe olives, drained
2 tablespoons olive or vegetable oil, divided
1/2 teaspoon dried oregano
2 tablespoons dry white wine or chicken broth
1 teaspoon sugar
1 teaspoon balsamic vinegar
1 garlic clove, minced
1/4 teaspoon dried thyme
1 medium onion, sliced

Directions

Flatten Chicken breasts to 1/8-in. thickness; set aside. In a food processor or blender, combine the cheese, olives, 1 tablespoon oil and oregano; cover and process until mixture reaches a thick chunky paste consistency. Spread over chicken breasts; roll up and tuck in ends. Secure with a wooden toothpick.

In a bowl, combine wine or broth, sugar, vinegar, garlic, thyme and remaining oil. Pour into an ungreased 2-qt. baking dish. Top with onion. Place chicken over onion. Cover and bake at 350 degrees F for 30 minutes. Uncover and baste with pan juices. Bake 15-20 minutes longer or until chicken juices run clear.

Absolutely Fabulous Greek/House Dressing

Ingredients

1 1/2 quarts olive oil
1/3 cup garlic powder
1/3 cup dried oregano
1/3 cup dried basil
1/4 cup pepper
1/4 cup salt
1/4 cup onion powder
1/4 cup Dijon-style mustard
2 quarts red wine vinegar

Directions

In a very large container, mix together the olive oil, garlic powder, oregano, basil, pepper, salt, onion powder, and Dijon-style mustard. Pour in the vinegar, and mix vigorously until well blended. Store tightly covered at room temperature.

Grilled Mediterranean Greek Pizza with Sundried

Ingredients

1 (12 ounce) package al fresco® All Natural Sun Dried Tomato with Basil Chicken Sausage

1 (14 ounce) package baked pizza crust (such as Boboli)

2 tablespoons garlic flavored olive oil

2/3 cup pizza sauce

1 cup shredded Italian cheese blend, reduced fat

1/3 cup crumbled feta cheese with basil and tomato

1 1/2 teaspoons dried oregano

Directions

Preheat grill on medium setting.

Place sausages on an oiled grill rack, set 4 to 5 inches over heat. Grill, using the direct grill method, turning links with tongs, until cooked throughout, about 7 to 9 minutes or until the internal temperature reaches 165 degrees F. Cool slightly and cut into 1/4 to 1/2-inch slices.

Brush both sides of pizza crust with olive oil. Gently place pizza crust, top-side down on grill rack. Grill for 2 to 3 minutes until crust is warm. Turn crust over.

Quickly spread pizza sauce on cooked side of pizza crust, then arrange sliced sausage on top of crust. Sprinkle with cheese and oregano. Grill over direct medium heat. Cover with grill lid or tent with foil.

Grill for 8 to 10 minutes or until toppings are warm and cheese has melted. Cut into wedges and serve.

Greek Tomato Salad

Ingredients

1/4 cup red wine vinegar or cider vinegar
2 tablespoons olive oil
1 garlic clove, minced
1/2 teaspoon dried oregano
1/4 teaspoon dried basil 1/8 teaspoon sugar
1/8 teaspoon salt
1/8 teaspoon pepper
1 cup thinly sliced red onion, separated into rings
1/2 cup coarsely chopped green pepper
4 tomatoes, cut into 8 wedges
6 pitted ripe olives, halved
3 tablespoons crumbled feta cheese

Directions

In a bowl, whisk together the vinegar, oil, oregano, basil, sugar, salt and pepper. Add red onion and green pepper; toss to coat. Stir in tomatoes, olives and cheese. Cover and refrigerate for at least 1 hour. Serve with a slotted spoon.

Greek Stuffed Tomatoes

Ingredients

4 large ripe tomatoes
salt and pepper to taste
1 tablespoon olive oil
1 cucumber, peeled and diced
1/2 cup yogurt
8 ounces black Greek olives,
pitted and sliced
1/4 cup chopped fresh basil
1 teaspoon sugar
2 cups crumbled feta cheese
1/4 cup chopped fresh parsley

Directions

Preheat oven to 350 degrees F (175 degrees C).

Slice tomatoes in half, scoop out seeds, and place in a baking dish sliced-side up. Sprinkle with and salt and pepper . Bake for 5 minutes. Remove tomatoes from oven, drizzle with olive oil, and bake an additional 10 minutes.

While baking tomatoes, mix together cucumber, yogurt, olives, basil, and sugar. Stir in feta cheese. Season to taste with salt and pepper.

Remove tomatoes from oven, fill with cucumber mixture, and sprinkle with parsley. Serve immediately.

Greek Pasta Salad II

Ingredients

1 (16 ounce) package rotini pasta
1 (10 ounce) package frozen chopped spinach
3 tablespoons olive oil
3 cloves garlic, minced
7 ounces crumbled feta cheese
1 tablespoon dried dill weed
salt and pepper to taste

Directions

Bring a large pot of lightly salted water to a boil. Add pasta and cook for 8 to 10 minutes or until al dente; drain and reserve. Meanwhile, in a medium saucepan over medium heat, bring water to a boil. Add spinach and cook for 5 minutes or until spinach is tender; drain and reserve.

In a large pot over medium heat, warm olive oil and saute garlic until golden; add pasta and spinach and mix.

Remove from heat and let cool for ten minutes. Add feta and dill; mix well and serve.

Frozen Greek Yogurt

Ingredients

3 cups plain whole-milk Greek
yogurt
1 tablespoon lemon juice
5 tablespoons honey
10 chopped fresh mint leaves

Directions

Stir together the yogurt and lemon juice until smooth in a freezer-safe metal bowl. Combine the honey and mint in a small bowl. Pour the honey on top of the yogurt, then give the yogurt a few quick stirs so that the honey forms "ribbons" in the yogurt but is not blended in completely. Cover bowl and freeze for 1 to 2 hours.

Good for You Greek Salad

Ingredients

3 large ripe tomatoes, chopped
2 cucumbers, peeled and chopped
1 small red onion, chopped
1/4 cup olive oil
4 teaspoons lemon juice
1 1/2 teaspoons dried oregano
salt and pepper to taste
1 cup crumbled feta cheese
6 black Greek olives, pitted and sliced

Directions

In shallow salad bowl, or on serving platter, combine tomatoes, cucumber, and onion. Sprinkle with oil, lemon juice, oregano, and salt and pepper to taste. Sprinkle feta cheese and olives over salad. Serve.

Stuffed Bell Peppers, Greek Style

Ingredients

2 tablespoons extra virgin olive oil
1 1/4 cups onion, chopped
1 pound ground lamb
3/4 cup white rice
3/4 teaspoon salt
1/2 teaspoon ground black pepper
1/2 teaspoon dried mint, crushed
1 cup water
1/4 cup chopped fresh parsley to aste
1 (14.5 ounce) can chicken broth
1 (14.5 ounce) can petite diced tomatoes
6 green bell pepper, top removed, seeded

Directions

Preheat an oven to 350 degrees F (175 degrees C).

Heat the olive oil in a large skillet over medium-high heat. Stir in the onion and ground lamb; cook and stir until the onion is tender, and the meat is no longer pink, about 7 minutes. Stir in the rice, salt, black pepper, and mint; cook 5 minutes longer. Add the water and parsley. Reduce the heat to medium-low, and continue cooking and stirring until the water has been completely absorbed by the rice, about 15 minutes. Stir the chicken broth and diced tomatoes together in an oven-proof dish that will just fit the peppers. Scoop the lamb mixture into the bell peppers, and place them into the dish.

Bake in the preheated oven until the peppers are tender and the tomatoes are bubbly, about 45 minutes.

Greeked Zucchini

Ingredients

1 medium zucchini, halved and sliced
1/4 cup diced red onion
1/4 cup diced green bell pepper
2 (4 ounce) cans sliced black olives, drained
1/4 cup crumbled feta cheese
2 tablespoons Greek vinaigrette salad dressing
1/4 cup grape or cherry tomatoes, halved

Directions

Preheat oven to 350 degrees F (175 degrees C).

Spray a large piece of aluminum foil with nonstick cooking spray. Layer the zucchini, onion, pepper, and olives onto the center. Sprinkle with feta cheese, and drizzle with vinaigrette. Fold into a packet and seal the edges.

Bake in preheated oven until vegetables are tender, about 30 minutes. Open the foil packet, turn the oven onto Broil, and broil until the feta lightly browns. Add the grape tomatoes and serve.

Greek Steffotto

Ingredients

2 pounds lean beef chuck,
trimmed and cut into 1 inch cubes
1 pound fresh mushrooms
1/2 cup chopped onions
1 (6 ounce) can tomato paste
1 cup wine vinegar
1/2 cup packed brown sugar
2 cinnamon sticks
1/4 teaspoon ground cloves
salt to taste
ground black pepper to taste

Directions

Brown the chuck in a large pan.

Add mushrooms and onions to meat, and cook until soft. Transfer to an oven proof pan.

Mix together tomato paste, wine vinegar, and brown sugar. Pour this mixture over the meat and vegetables. Add cinnamon sticks, sprinkle of whole cloves, and salt and pepper to taste. Dilute with water to cover all.

Bake at 325 degrees F (165 degrees C) for at least 2 to 2 1/2 hours.

My Big Fat Greek Omelet

Ingredients

1 cup halved grape tomatoes
1 teaspoon dried oregano, divided
1/2 teaspoon salt, divided
Black pepper, to taste
1/2 cup crumbled feta cheese (can use reduced-fat)
8 large eggs
1 (10 ounce) package chopped frozen spinach, thawed and squeezed dry
1 tablespoon olive oil

Directions

Heat a 12-inch non-stick skillet over low heat. (Use a 10-inch skillet if you halve the recipe to serve 2 instead of 4.) Meanwhile, in a small bowl, mix tomatoes, 1/2 tsp. oregano, 1/4 tsp. salt, and pepper to taste. Stir in feta.

In a medium bowl, whisk eggs together, then stir in spinach, 1/2 tsp. oregano, 1/4 tsp. salt, and pepper to taste. A few minutes before cooking omelet, add oil to the pan, and increase heat to medium-high. Heat until wisps of smoke start to rise from the pan. Add the egg mixture to the skillet. Using a plastic or wooden spatula to push back the eggs that have set, tilt the pan and let the uncooked egg mixture run onto the empty portion of the pan. Continue pushing back cooked eggs, tilting the pan and letting uncooked egg mixture flow onto the empty portion of the pan until omelet is moist but fully cooked, about 3 minutes. Reduce heat to low; pour the tomato mixture over half of the omelet. Using a slotted, flat spatula or turner, carefully fold the untopped half over the filling. Use the turner to slide the omelet onto a cutting board. Let stand a minute or two for the filling to warm.

Cut the omelet into 4 wedges and serve immediately.

Greek Green Beans

Ingredients

3/4 cup olive oil
2 cups chopped onions
1 clove garlic, minced
2 pounds fresh green beans,
rinsed and trimmed
3 large tomatoes, diced
2 teaspoons sugar
salt to taste

Directions

Heat the olive oil in a large skillet over medium heat. Cook and stir the onions and garlic in the skillet until tender.

Mix the green beans, tomatoes, sugar, and salt into the skillet. Reduce heat to low, and continue cooking 45 minutes, or until beans are soft.

Greek Shrimp Dish From Santorini

Ingredients

1/4 cup butter
2 tablespoons garlic, minced
1 bunch flat-leaf parsley, chopped
2 pints grape tomatoes, halved
1/2 (750 milliliter) bottle dry white wine
2 pounds peeled and deveined medium shrimp
1 (4 ounce) container crumbled feta cheese
2 lemons, halved
2 sprigs fresh flat-leaf parsley

Directions

Melt the butter in a saucepan over medium heat. Stir in the garlic, chopped parsley, tomatoes, and wine. Bring to a simmer, then reduce heat to medium-low, and cook for 1 hour, stirring occasionally, until the sauce has slightly thickened.

Preheat oven to 250 degrees F (120 degrees C).

Stir the shrimp into the tomato sauce, and cook for 2 minutes; remove from the heat. Pour the shrimp mixture into a shallow baking dish, and sprinkle with crumbled feta cheese. Bake in the preheated oven until the feta has softened and the shrimp are no longer translucent, 45 minutes to 1 hour. Squeeze the lemon halves over the shrimp and garnish with the parsley sprigs to serve.

Kourambiathes (Greek Cookies)

Ingredients

1 cup butter
1 egg yolk
2 tablespoons anise extract
1/4 cup confectioners' sugar
2 1/2 cups all-purpose flour
1/3 cup confectioners' sugar for dusting

Directions

Preheat oven to 350 degrees F (175 degrees C). Grease cookie sheets.

In a medium bowl, cream the butter, egg yolk and anise extract until light. Stir in the 1/4 cup confectioners' sugar and flour until blended.

Shape dough into crescents and place 2 inches apart on the prepared baking sheets. Bake for 15 to 20 minutes in the preheated oven. Dust heavily with confectioners' sugar before they are completely cool.

George's Greek Fried Chicken

Ingredients

4 skinless chicken pieces
1/2 cup Greek olive oil
1 lemon, juiced
1 1/2 tablespoons freshly ground black pepper
1 teaspoon salt
1 1/2 tablespoons dried oregano
1 dash cinnamon
1 dash poultry seasoning
1/2 cup olive oil for frying
1 lemon, cut into wedges

Directions

In a medium bowl, combine chicken pieces with 1/2 cup olive oil, lemon juice, pepper, salt, oregano, cinnamon, and poultry seasoning. Allow the chicken to soak in the oil and seasonings for five minutes. In fact, rub the marinade into the chicken using your hands.

Heat 1/2 cup olive oil over low heat in a 1 1/2 inch deep frying pan with a lid to fit (to keep the juices in the chicken). Carefully lay the chicken pieces in the frying pan. Put the lid on the pan, and cook until chicken is done, about 20 minutes, flipping pieces occasionally. Increase heat to medium-high, and cook just long enough to make the outside of the chicken brown.

Serve hot, garnished with lemon wedges. Squeeze some lemon on the chicken for delicious added flavor.

Greek Saganaki

Ingredients

8 ounces feta cheese
1 egg
1 teaspoon finely chopped fresh oregano
1/2 cup all-purpose flour
2 tablespoons olive oil
freshly ground black pepper
2 large ripe tomatoes, sliced
1 lemon, cut into wedges

Directions

Slice feta into 2x3/8 inch squares, about 8 slices. In a small bowl, beat the egg with the oregano. Dip each slice of feta in egg, shake off excess, and coat in flour.

Heat olive oil in a frying pan over medium heat. Quickly cook cheese in olive oil until golden, turning once. Pat dry with paper towels.

Arrange feta on a plate with thick tomato slices, season with black pepper, and garnish with lemon wedges.

Greek Feta And Olive Spread

Ingredients

1 (6 ounce) package feta cheese, crumbled
2 tablespoons olive oil
1 teaspoon lemon juice
1/2 teaspoon minced garlic
2 ounces sun-dried tomatoes, softened
1/2 teaspoon dried oregano
1 tablespoon chopped black olives, drained

Directions

In a food processor, place the feta cheese, olive oil, lemon juice, garlic, sun-dried tomatoes and oregano. Using the pulse setting, blend the mixture until smooth. Transfer to a medium bowl. Blend in the olives by hand or with a spoon. Refrigerate until serving.

Greek Lamb Kabobs

Ingredients

1/2 cup lemon juice
2 tablespoons dried oregano
4 teaspoons olive oil
5 garlic cloves, minced
1 pound lean lamb, trimmed of fat and cut into 1 inch cubes
16 cherry tomatoes
1 large green pepper, cut into 1-inch pieces
1 large onion, cut into 1-inch wedges

Directions

In a small bowl, combine the lemon juice, oregano, oil and garlic. Set aside 1/4 cup for basting; cover and refrigerate. Pour the remaining marinade into a large resealable plastic bag; add the lamb. Seal bag and turn to coat; refrigerate for 8 hours or overnight, turning occasionally.

Coat grill rack with nonstick cooking spray before starting the grill. Drain and discard marinade. On eight metal or soaked wooden skewers, alternately thread lamb, tomatoes, green pepper and onion. Grill kabobs, uncovered, over medium heat for 3 minutes on each side. Baste with reserved marinade. Grill 8-10 minutes longer or until meat reaches desired doneness, turning and basting frequently.

Two Layer Greek Dip

Ingredients

2 (8 ounce) containers plain yogurt
1 (8 ounce) package cream cheese, softened
1 (8 ounce) package feta cheese, drained and crumbled
3 cloves garlic, crushed
salt and pepper to taste
1 English cucumber, peeled and diced
5 roma (plum) tomatoes, seeded and chopped
5 green onions, chopped
1 (4 ounce) can sliced black olives
black pepper to taste
pita bread rounds, cut into triangles

Directions

In a bowl, stir together the yogurt, softened cream cheese, feta cheese, garlic, and salt and pepper to taste; mix until smooth.

Spread mixture into a shallow serving or baking dish. Cover, and refrigerate for 3 hours, or overnight.

To serve, scatter cucumber, tomatoes, green onion, and sliced olives on top, and season with pepper as desired. Spoon onto pita wedges.

Herbed Greek Roasted Potatoes with Feta Cheese

Ingredients

5 pounds potatoes, cut into wedges
6 cloves garlic, minced
3/4 cup olive oil
1 cup water
1/4 cup fresh lemon juice
sea salt to taste
ground black pepper to taste
1 1/2 tablespoons dried oregano
1 teaspoon chopped fresh mint
1 (8 ounce) package crumbled feta cheese

Directions

Preheat an oven to 450 degrees F (230 degrees C). Lightly oil a large baking dish.

Stir the potatoes, garlic, olive oil, water, lemon juice, salt, and pepper together in a bowl until the potatoes are evenly coated; pour into the prepared baking dish.

Roast in the preheated oven until the potatoes begin to brown, about 40 minutes. Season the potatoes with the oregano and mint. If the dish appears dry, pour another 1/2 cup water into the dish. Return to the oven and bake about 40 minutes more. Top with the crumbled feta cheese to serve.

Greek Pasta Salad III

Ingredients

8 ounces rotini pasta
1/2 cup olive oil
1/2 cup red wine vinegar
1 1/2 teaspoons garlic powder
1 1/2 teaspoons dried basil leaves
1 1/2 teaspoons dried oregano
3 cups sliced mushrooms
15 halved cherry tomatoes
3/4 cup crumbled feta cheese
1/2 cup chopped green onions
1 (4 ounce) can chopped black olives

Directions

Bring a large pot of lightly salted water to a boil. Add rotini pasta and cook for 8 to 10 minutes or until al dente; drain.

Mix together cooked pasta, olive oil, vinegar, garlic powder, basil, oregano, mushrooms, tomatoes, Feta cheese, green onions and olives. Cover and chill for at least 2 hours, serve cold.

Greek Seasoning

Ingredients

1 1/2 teaspoons dried oregano
1 teaspoon dried mint
1 teaspoon dried thyme
1/2 teaspoon dried basil
1/2 teaspoon dried marjoram
1/2 teaspoon dried minced onion
1/4 teaspoon dried minced garlic

Directions

In a small bowl, combine all ingredients. Store in an airtight container in a cool dry place for up to 6 months.

Greek God Pasta

Ingredients

1 (16 ounce) package whole wheat rotini pasta
1 (16 ounce) can peeled and diced tomatoes, drained
2 tablespoons chopped green bell pepper
1/4 cup chopped green onion
3 cups tomato sauce
1 teaspoon dried basil
1 teaspoon dried oregano
1 cup sliced black olives
1/2 cup shredded mozzarella cheese
2 tablespoons crumbled feta cheese

Directions

Preheat the oven to 400 degrees F (200 degrees C).

Bring a large pot of lightly salted water to a boil. Add rotini pasta, and cook until al dente, about 8 minutes. Drain and pour into a deep casserole dish.

Stir tomatoes, green pepper, green onion, olives and tomato sauce into the pasta. Season with basil and oregano and mix until evenly blended. Sprinkle mozzarella and feta cheese over the top.

Bake for 30 minutes in the preheated oven, until cheese is melted and bubbly. Let stand for a few minutes before serving.

Greek Sausage: Sheftalia

Ingredients

1 pound ground pork
1 large onion, finely chopped
1/2 cup finely chopped fresh parsley
1 pinch salt and pepper to taste
1 tablespoon vinegar
1/2 pound caul fat
10 skewers

Directions

In a medium bowl, mix together the ground pork, onion, parsley, salt and pepper.

Fill a bowl with warm water, and add the vinegar. Dip the caul fat into the water, and keep submerged for 1 minute to wash. Rinse in cold water. Carefully open up the caul fat on a clean work surface, and cut into 4 inch (10 cm) squares.

Place a small compressed handful of the sausage near the edge of one square. Fold the sides over, and roll up firmly. Repeat with remaining meat and fat until you have about 10 sausages.

Prepare a charcoal grill for high heat. Place sausages onto skewers.

Grill the sausages for 20 minutes, turning frequently until the outside is crispy and dark, and the inside is no longer pink.

Greek-Style Stuffed Peppers

Ingredients

4 large green bell peppers, tops removed, seeded
4 large red bell peppers, tops removed, seeded
1 tablespoon olive oil
1/2 pound ground pork
2 onions, chopped
salt and pepper to taste
1/4 cup dry white wine
1 (10.75 ounce) can tomato puree
1 (4 ounce) package feta cheese
1/2 cup cooked white rice
1/2 cup raisins
1/2 cup pine nuts
2 tablespoons chopped fresh parsley

Directions

Preheat oven to 350 degrees F (175 degrees C). Place green and red bell peppers in a bowl with enough warm water to cover, and soak 5 minutes.

Heat the olive oil in a skillet over medium heat. Place pork and onions in the skillet, season with salt and pepper, and cook until pork is evenly brown. Drain grease, and mix in wine and tomato puree. Continue cooking 10 minutes.

Transfer skillet mixture to a large bowl, and mix in feta cheese, cooked rice, raisins, pine nuts, and parsley. Stuff peppers with the mixture, and arrange in a baking dish. Cover with aluminum foil.

Bake 30 minutes in the preheated oven. Remove foil, and continue baking 10 minutes, until stuffing is lightly browned. May be served hot or cold.

Cousin Cosmo's Greek Chicken

Ingredients

2 tablespoons all-purpose flour, divided
1/2 teaspoon salt
1/4 teaspoon black pepper
1/4 pound feta cheese, crumbled
1 tablespoon fresh lemon juice
1 teaspoon dried oregano
6 boneless, skinless chicken breast halves
2 tablespoons olive oil
1 1/2 cups water
1 cube chicken bouillon, crumbled
2 cups loosely packed torn fresh spinach leaves
1 ripe tomato, chopped

Directions

On large plate, combine 1 tablespoon flour, salt, and pepper. Set aside. In a small bowl, combine cheese, lemon juice, and oregano. Set aside.

With a meat mallet, pound each chicken breast to 1/2 inch thickness. Spread cheese mixture on each chicken breast, leaving 1/2 inch border. Fold chicken breasts in half; secure each with toothpick. Coat chicken breasts with flour mixture.

In large skillet, heat oil over medium heat. Cook chicken breasts for 1 to 2 minutes on each side, until golden. In a small bowl, whisk together 1 1/2 cups water, chicken bouillon cube, and remaining flour; pour over chicken breasts in pan. Add spinach and tomato to skillet, and bring to boil. Cover, reduce heat to low, and simmer for 8 to 10 minutes, or until chicken is no longer pink inside. Discard toothpicks before serving.

Greek Orzo Salad

Ingredients

1 cup uncooked orzo pasta
2 cups frozen corn, thawed
1/2 cup chopped sweet red pepper
1/2 cup grape or cherry tomatoes
1/2 cup pitted Greek olives, halved
1/4 cup chopped sweet onion
1/4 cup minced fresh basil
2 tablespoons minced fresh parsley
3 tablespoons olive oil
2 tablespoons balsamic vinegar
1/4 teaspoon salt
1/4 teaspoon pepper

Directions

Cook pasta according to package directions; drain and rinse in cold water. Place in a large serving bowl; add the corn, red pepper, tomatoes, olives, onion, basil and parsley. In a jar with a tight-fitting lid, combine the oil, vinegar, salt and pepper; shake well. Pour over salad and toss to coat. Yield: 8 servings.

CPSIA information can be obtained
at www.ICGtesting.com
Printed in the USA
LVHW060826100221
678895LV00002BA/139